The Road to
Forgiveness

The Road to
Forgiveness

Nancy Eichman

Gospel Advocate Company
Nashville, Tennessee

Published by Gospel Advocate Co.
1006 Elm Hill Pike, Nashville, TN 37210
http://www.gospeladvocate.com

ISBN: 0-89225-552-8

To the Faculty, Staff and Student Workers of
Brackett Library, Harding University, Searcy, Ark. –

some of the most God-loving
people-loving, fun-loving people I know.

God bless you!

Hugs to my family for their love and support –
my children, John and Amy, and especially
my husband, Phil, for his editorial help.

Mapping Out the Trip

Introduction: What a Road Trip! ... 9

Part One: Choosing the Best Route ... 11

Chapter 1 Which Way Is Forgiveness? 13
What If They Meant No Harm? 21

Chapter 2 Preparing for the Trip 23
Are Some People Too Bad to Forgive? 30

Chapter 3 Following the Signs............................... 31
What Does God Do With Our Sins? 38

Chapter 4 Beyond Road Rage 39
Why Did Jesus Assert His Authority to Forgive Sins? 46

Chapter 5 Going Beyond the Expected 47
Did Jesus Give the Apostles the Power to Forgive Sins? 54

Part Two: Getting Around the Obstacles ... 55

Chapter 6 You Can't Get There From Here..................... 57
If Jesus Died for Everyone, Why Isn't Everyone Saved? 63

Chapter 7 Shedding Your Baggage 65
How Can We Forget a Minor Offense Against Us? 72

Chapter 8 Maneuvering Around the Potholes 73
Do Flashbacks Mean I Am Not Forgiven? 81

Chapter 9 Lost and Going in Circles 83
Does God Give Up on the Wicked? 90

Part Three: On the Road Again ... 91

Chapter 10 Making a U-Turn................................. 93
What If They Just Won't Listen?.................... 101

Chapter 11 Patching Things Up............................... 103
Does God Really Forget Our Sins?................... 110

Chapter 12   Restoring Something Worth Saving 111
             Was There Complete Forgiveness
             in the Old Testament? 119

Chapter 13   The Last Few Miles. 121
             How Do I Know If I Have Truly Forgiven Someone? 129

A Prayer of Forgiveness 131

Endnotes 133

Introduction

What a Road Trip!

A re you ready for a road trip? I'm not talking about the cross-coun-
try, Maine to California variety. Rather I'm envisioning a very
difficult journey with some roadblocks, breakdowns, and maybe even
some dead ends along the way. It won't be easy but it will certainly be
worth the trip.

I'm talking about taking the road to forgiveness. You will need to take
it if anyone has ever hurt you. Although the offense might have happened years ago, you may still feel the pain as though it were yesterday.

Or maybe you have hurt someone. You didn't mean to – or maybe
you did. You suffer from the burden of guilt and loss of a broken relationship. You want to make things better but you don't know how.
Perhaps you have given up and consider reconciliation impossible.

Possibly you feel you can never forgive.

Or you feel you could never be forgiven.

The road to forgiveness is a road everyone must take to get to heaven.
There are no detours, no less-traveled shortcuts to skip the important
stops during the journey. We might not want to take this route often but
it is the only way to get to where we need to be.

We can take comfort in knowing the route has already been mapped
out for us. Numerous fellow wanderers have traveled before us. It wasn't
easy for them either. Some never made it. But others arrived at their

destination, even though they grew weary of the journey. They did it, and so can we.

The one who drew up our map has been on the road so many times that He knows the way well. God, our Navigator, can direct our path by the best map available – the Bible. Through its illuminating pages, we can learn about the ultimate plan in which Jesus, His Son, made it possible for us to be forgiven through His grace and how we can extend forgiveness to others – and to ourselves.

That's what we hope to explore in this book – forgiving and being forgiven. In life we are called to do both. The road to forgiveness is a process, a journey. It takes time. It cannot be rushed. It involves making side trips, clearing the obstacles, and sometimes even getting lost and finding the way back. We might even wonder if it is worth the trip.

So join me on this journey. We can learn to do what many people have thought impossible – to forgive. We can know the joy of forgiving and being forgiven. What a road trip it can be!

Part One

Choosing the Best Route

In Bible times, travelers found their way by the stars. In the early days of the American West, they sent a seasoned pathfinder to scout out the best route for the wagon train. Later, with the availability of maps, reliable transportation, and paved highways, vacationers could plot out their trip and plan overnight stops. Now, with the advent of the Internet, the savvy mapster can input her starting point and her destination and in a few minutes print off the best route according to that map website.

But leave it to technology to find an even more innovative way to find the best route. If you would rather hear your directions instead of fumbling with paper maps, you have another alternative. A GPS system in your vehicle knows where you are at all times because it has satellite-reading capability. It can tell you when and where to make turns and can also help you find ATMs, restaurants and hotels. Type in your destination and a voice starts you on your way with directions also being displayed on a screen. If you miss your turn, no problem. The voice directs you back on course. It is a rather expensive alternative to paper maps, but then again, maps can't talk! [1]

Fortunately, we have a Navigator who knows where we are all the time. We need to learn the way to forgiveness and, with Him, we can know we are on the right road. He can direct us to our destination, utilizing the best route. We need only to check out His map: the Bible.

Chapter 1

Which Way Is Forgiveness?

"Saying 'I forgive' is like taking an emotional shower –
forgiveness cleanses and frees the entrapped soul."
~ Don Colbert [1]

A mother once caught her little boy munching his favorite cookies right before dinner. With little remorse he nonchalantly handed her the depleted bag and stated, "I should ask forgiveness, shouldn't I, Mom?"

"Only if you are sorry," she replied.

"Why be sorry? I love eating those cookies. Being sorry would be dumb!" [2]

Forgiveness doesn't always make sense! It is not easy to understand and even more difficult to accomplish. Many people, including Christians, misunderstand what forgiveness means, how we reach it, and why anyone would even want to forgive in the first place. They wonder, "How can I forgive?"

You have probably asked the same question – "How can I forgive? How can I ever let go of the pain that he has caused? After what she has done, how can I just pardon her?" Or we might be flooded with pain from our own guilt of hurting others, thinking, "How can they ever forgive me? How can I forgive myself after what I have done?" Maybe we look at ourselves in shame and wonder how God can ever forgive us.

Some people resist, even refuse to forgive because they misunderstand what forgiveness is. To help us understand what it involves, we need to know what forgiveness is not.

What Forgiveness Is Not

• *Forgiveness is not condoning evil.* Forgiveness is not making a wrong right just by saying, "It doesn't matter; I forgive you." Genuine forgiveness is more like, "It does matter. Some things might never be the same. But I will forgive you anyway." Forgiveness doesn't trivialize evil nor does it condone or tolerate the sin that was committed. It doesn't discount the consequences resulting from that sin. Justice demands that a penalty be paid. Sometimes the government, which is God-ordained, must administer that penalty (Romans 13:1-4). The arsonist must make restitution for damages he inflicted. The rapist must complete his sentence in prison. The church treasurer who embezzled church funds must repay what he stole and be relieved of his position. All these offenders may receive mercy by being forgiven by their victims and by God, but justice demands they suffer consequences for their crimes. [3]

• *Forgiveness is not excusing the offender.* Many of us feel that if we forgive someone who hurt us, then we are excusing the person. For example, a mother whose daughter was killed in a store burglary might refuse to forgive the offender because she thinks if she does, it will excuse him and defame her daughter's memory.

When we forgive someone, it does not mean we make excuses for her behavior. Excusing takes the responsibility away from the person saying she is not to blame for the offense. If there is no one to blame, then there is no need to forgive. Forgiving, on the other hand, puts the responsibility for the wrong squarely on the offending person's shoulders. [4]

• *Forgiveness is not avoiding conflict.* Some people will do anything to avoid confrontation, even if it means sweeping dirty problems under the rug of propriety. It's true that Jesus commended peacemakers (Matthew 5:9) and Paul admonished us to "live at peace with everyone" (Romans 12:18). But there are times when problems need to be dealt with, even to the point of conflict, so they can be addressed and possibly solved. For example, family members may gloss over the mother's alcoholism by saying, "We'll just forgive her and go on." They are only postponing dealing with the real issue. Smothering conflict sometimes makes forgiveness ultimately more difficult to accomplish. [5]

• *Forgivness is not compensating the good for the bad.* We

do not have to find some redeeming quality that makes the offender worth forgiving. A good trait (or several, for that matter) does not make up for the injury that was done. One does not even out the other. A person's good behavior at one time does not negate the hurt that took place another time. Forgiveness is not a method of balancing the scales. [6]

• *Forgivness is not forgetting.* We have been taught the adage, "Forgive and forget." Some might equate the two actions, but they are not the same. Trying to forget and act as if the wrong never happened will not make it go away. Only by remembering the injury in the first place can we begin to forgive the one who hurt us.

Forgiving can facilitate the forgetting process. After true forgiveness takes place, we can begin to feel free to heal from the past and forget the wrong. We might still remember it but not in the same way. For instance, a worker might never fully forget a coworker's thoughtless and unwarranted criticism of her work, but with time and forgiveness, she can learn to let it fade from her heart. [7]

• *Forgiveness is not just "making up."* Were you ever asked to "shake hands and make up" when you got into a fight as a child? While this may or may not have worked to mend your childhood squabbles, adults need to do more to forgive than an obligatory handshake. Sadly though, adults may give the appearance of forgiving and making peace but underneath the facade is a bitter, unforgiving spirit. Take, for example, a quarrel between members in the church. They give the appearance of getting along and forgiving but are only appeasing the preacher when he's looking! There is definitely more to genuine forgiveness.

So what is genuine forgiveness? How do we start our journey to reach it? And why is it so important to Christians? God's Word has the answers.

What Forgiveness Means

If we look at the New Testament, we find the root meaning of one word for forgiveness is "to release" or "to let go" of an obligation. This could refer to a marriage contract or job, but it commonly was used for canceling a financial obligation. Jesus often used this meaning to illustrate the concept of forgiveness, especially in His parables. [8]

For example, in Matthew 18:23-35, Jesus told a parable about a king who called for his accounts to be cleared. He found one servant owed him an exorbitant sum – millions of dollars in today's currency. When the servant couldn't repay his debt, the king promptly ordered him, his family, and all he had to be sold. The servant begged on his knees for more time to pay it all back. The king, moved with compassion, canceled his debt and freed him from his obligations.

This is a prime example of forgiveness. Look first at how the king forgave the servant's debt. The lender (king) had the legal right to get his money back. The borrower (servant) was obligated to repay. Out of mercy, the king canceled the debt and covered the loss himself. [9]

How does this play out when we forgive someone else? First we recognize that some wrong has been committed. Next we acknowledge that this wrong requires repayment. Then we choose to cover the entire loss ourselves, thus releasing the offender's obligation to us. Note that it does not erase his debt or obligation. Rather we take the debt onto ourselves instead of him. [10]

Usually we don't have trouble remembering how we have been wronged and what obligation is needed to make it right. Somehow our memory can remember those little details for years! It is the last part – the forgiving or releasing of hurt and wrong – that proves to be the hardest. Why would anyone want to release someone else's obligation and take it upon herself? [11]

Why Forgive?

• *Forgiveness settles the debt.* In the previous parable, even if the king had carried through with his plan to sell the servant, his family and all their belongings, he would never recoup the exorbitant debt. Essentially, the servant would be hard-pressed to repay the debt in his lifetime. The servant in no way deserved the king's generous offer to cancel his debt.

In the same way, we do not deserve to be forgiven when we do wrong. Can we ever really undo the damage that has been done to another person? We can try to made amends for what we have done. But the thoughtless word, the unkind gesture, the careless act, the malicious deed, even the unintentional hurt – all have passed into eternity and cannot be taken back. Even for slight offenses, there is still some loss – maybe inconvenience, embarrassment and loss of time or money. Can even these be replaced? We cannot undo what we have done. By ourselves we can never pay back the debts of our sins.

Only through an act of grace do we receive forgiveness from God or from each other. Though defined in many ways, we understand grace as unmerited favor. When someone forgives, she clearly understands she was wronged but forgives anyway. Forgiveness is undeserved, no matter what the restitution, remorse or penance. Forgiveness releases us of the "debtor's prison" of guilt and bitterness. It settles the debt as nothing else can. [12]

• *Forgiveness frees us to move on.* Not only does forgiveness free us from the debt of sin, but it also frees us to get on with our lives. A lack of forgiveness stalemates us to one point in time when we rehearse the injury over and over again. Forgiveness allows us to get beyond that point. Instead of being stuck on an event in the past, we can look to the future with a free heart.

In collecting his debts, the king of the parable probably wanted to get his many affairs of state in order. He realized he didn't need to be encumbered with the debt of a servant who couldn't pay it back anyway. So the king decided to cut his losses, forgive the entire debt, and clear his books.

Have you ever loaned money to a good friend who promises to get it back to you – but never does? The money means a lot to you, but your friendship means more. Eventually you might get to the point where you say, "I'll never see that money again anyway. I'm going to forget the debt and move on with my life. Our friendship is not worth destroying over some money."

Some might say that canceling the debt and moving on is a selfish motive. They say it focuses on making you feel better. But Paul exhorts us not to let anything encumber us in our Christian growth (Romans 12:1-2). We must move ahead toward the future instead of getting mired in the events of the past. [13] Like someone once quipped, "Letting go of a rattlesnake might help the snake but it benefits you as well." [14]

• *Forgiveness avoids needless pain.* Unforgiveness extends the pain. Unforgiveness causes bitterness, resentment, anger and sorrow. It poisons the soul just as a foreign object poisons the body. People who refuse to forgive imprison themselves in their own personal torture chamber with a lifetime sentence of needless suffering.

That's what eventually happened to the first servant in the parable. How relieved he was to be forgiven by the king. But then he remembered that another servant owed him a few dollars (in today's currency). He demanded his fellow servant repay this paltry amount and even started choking him! When the second servant was unable to repay, he was thrown into prison until he could. [15]

When the other servants informed the king of the first servant's treatment of the second, the king had the unforgiving servant handed over to the jailers where he was tortured, probably to find if there were any hidden assets to use for payment. There he was kept until he should repay all the debt. Prison was worse than slavery for paying back debts in that culture, especially for this servant. Because he had fallen out of favor with the king, no allies would likely rise to help him. These friends were probably his only hope for getting out of debt and prison. [16]

There is so much needless suffering because of unforgiveness. We have a choice to forgive, move on and be better; or we can refuse to let go of our hard feelings and be bitter. The writer of Hebrews warns us against this vice: "See to it that no one misses the grace of God and that no bitter root grows up to cause trouble and defile many" (Hebrews 12:15). Bitterness not only infects us but also those around us. Author Frederick Buechner wrote about the consequences of an unforgiving spirit:

> To lick your wounds, to smack your lips over grievances long past, to roll over your tongue the prospect of bitter confrontations still to come, to savor to the last toothsome morsel both the pain you are given and the pain you are giving back – in many ways it is a feast fit for a king. The chief drawback is that what you are wolfing down is yourself. The skeleton at the feast is you. [17]

• *Forgiveness obligates us to forgive.* The parable of the unforgiving servant shows an inseparable connection between receiving and giving forgiveness. Even the servants saw that their fellow servant was unjustified in his demand to be repaid when he had been forgiven so much. They could not help reporting to the king the inequity they saw. In wrapping up the parable, no wonder Jesus drove the point home when

He emphasized, "This is how my heavenly Father will treat each of you unless you forgive your brother from your heart" (Matthew 18:35).

We understand that the king in the parable represents God and the servants represent us. Whatever pain we have experienced from the wrongdoing of others, it is minuscule compared to the sins we have committed against God. While we owe God such a great debt – millions of dollars – how can we refuse to forgive our fellow man who owes us just a few dollars? [18]

Which way is forgiveness? It's time to hit the road and find out. First we need to figure out what we need to take for the trip there – and what we don't need. Start packing!

Stopping to Ask

1. What is the danger in believing that forgiveness really condones or excuses sin?

2. Whom did God ordain to administer justice and penalties for crime (Romans 13:1-4)?

3. How can confrontation be healthy in working toward forgiveness?

4. How can forgiving facilitate forgetting?

5. Why is genuine forgiveness not the same as a forced "shaking hands and making up"?

6. How did Jesus use the concept of canceling a debt in Matthew 18:23-35 and Luke 7:41-43 to demonstrate forgiveness?

7. In the Old Testament what provisions were made for debtors being sold as slaves to pay their debts (Leviticus 25:39-43; 2 Kings 4:1)? Who disregarded this (Job 24:9; Nehemiah 5:1-13)?

8. How does forgiveness help us get on with our lives?

9. Why do unforgiving people hurt themselves the most?

10. Why does God's forgiveness obligate us to forgive others?

Going Further – 2 Samuel 13

1. What was Amnon's plan to seduce his half-sister Tamar? What happened as a result?

2. What was King David's reaction to Tamar's disgrace? How did David deal with Amnon's sin? Given his own past, why do you think David dealt with Amnon's sin the way he did?

3. What was the punishment for a man guilty of rape or a man having sexual relations with his sister as stipulated by the Law of Moses (Exodus 22:16; Leviticus 20:17, 19; Deuteronomy 22:28-29)?

4. What was the eventual result of Amnon's lust?

5. Why is acknowledgment of sin an important part of forgiveness? Have you ever not dealt with sin and then seen its damaging effects?

What If They Meant No Harm?

The whole idea of forgiveness seems to assume that someone is always guilty of wrongdoing. But what if the wrongdoer had no intention of hurting anyone? What if he does not even know any harm occurred? Do we still need to forgive him?

It often helps to ask first, "Have I really been hurt?" Our perception is important even if it is one-sided. If we think we have been offended, then we think someone is guilty of hurting us – even if that person did not mean for it to happen.

For example, a 5-year-old might not understand if his parents said they would take him to the circus but then must cancel to take his grandmother to the hospital. The parents did nothing wrong, but the son might not make that distinction. He will still be hurt and angry. The parents can say they are sorry and promise to take him somewhere special at another time. The child's feelings are then acknowledged.[19] The same is true when we hurt the feelings of a friend. Perhaps she takes offense when we meant none. The fact remains that she is hurt. To clear the air, we should apologize. Isn't it worth our friendship to say, "I'm sorry"?

People can be hurt seriously by someone intending no harm. The pain is still very real. We may find ourselves in situations that call for forgiveness, even if the offender is "objectively innocent."[20] For example, a widow mourns the loss of her husband who was in an accident at work that was nobody's fault. Although she knows nothing could have been done to prevent it, she still feels angry with her husband for leaving her alone. As she works through her grief, in time she can forgive him.

To give us perspective, it is interesting to note that the Law of Moses distinguished between one who sinned unintentionally and one who sinned willfully. The defiant sinner was cut off from the people because his guilt remained (Numbers 15:22-31). The person who unintentionally sinned was considered guilty, but atonement could be made through a specified offering (Leviticus 4). Deuteronomy 4:41-42 shows us that God was more merciful in His judgment to those who had accidentally killed someone: "Then Moses set aside three cities east of the Jordan, to which anyone who had killed a person could flee if he had unintentionally killed his neighbor without malice aforethought."

Chapter 2

Preparing for the Trip

"Everyone says forgiveness is a lovely idea
until they have something to forgive."
~ C.S. Lewis [1]

When I have the opportunity to go on a road trip, I'm ready to go – in mind, that is! But those little details like packing, preparing the house, and checking the car can put a damper on my enthusiasm. When I want to go, I want to go now! But if I don't take the time to prepare, I might find myself with no extra clothes, a clogged mailbox, and a flat tire!

What to Expect

For someone who loves to travel, I really hate to pack! Even with lighter rolling luggage, travel-size shampoo, and see-through zippered plastic bags, I still dread that travel necessity. The thing that makes it so difficult for me is the decision making. What clothes will be needed for what occasion? How about the weather? How much is too much? Will I end up looking like a rumpled rat?

What really helps me in this packing dilemma is knowing what I can expect from the trip. What will the journey involve? The same is true with the trip to forgiveness. What is a journey to forgiveness like?

• *Unique.* Just as our life experiences are unique, so each of us goes through the process of forgiveness differently. Each situation involving forgiveness is different. We cannot say, "I've been through a situation just like that" because we haven't. Maybe our situation is similar, but it is not the same. Forgiveness is personal. It is not a rigid, calculated process through which everyone follows the same steps.

• *Complex.* Forgiveness is complex because relationships are complex and multifaceted. Even with the best of intentions, misunderstandings and hurt feelings occur. Often blame is not one-sided. Destructive layers of hurt and distrust can build up between people. Just like an onion, these layers need to be peeled away one by one to enable one to forgive.

• *Difficult.* While forgiveness can at times be easier than we think, it is not a simple answer to fix a tangled mass of relational problems. Often it can involve deep pain and introspective soul-searching. Forgiveness stretches our emotional muscles. It should be understood for the serious work it is. [2] After all, something so crucial as forgiveness should not be approached lightly or superficially. [3]

• *Divine.* Poet Alexander Pope wrote, "To err is human, to forgive divine." [4] Pope had the right idea. The very divine nature of God is characterized by love and forgiveness. The Levites in Nehemiah described the Lord like this: "But you are a forgiving God, gracious and compassionate, slow to anger and abounding in love" (Nehemiah 9:17). We emulate that divine gift of freely given forgiveness when we forgive someone. Some people think that forgiveness is impossible in some situations. That might be true of ourselves, but we need to go beyond ourselves and ask for God's help. He can help us do what we thought was impossible (Ephesians 3:20; Matthew 19:26).

What to Leave Behind

If you have ever packed too many of the wrong kind of clothes for a trip, you know the frustration of wasting valuable space in place of something that was really needed. In a similar way, some qualities are necessary for forgiveness while others are better left behind. Knowing ahead of time what the journey will be like helps us know what not to bring.

• *Unrealistic Expectations.* Forget the Superman cape! We cannot reach forgiveness, resolving all pain and wrongdoing, with a single bound. Neither does every trip culminate with a happy ending. While we can control our own actions, it is unrealistic to think we can control what someone else does. We cannot force another person to forgive us; neither can we afterwards build a relationship with one who doesn't desire it.

• *Inflexibility.* Leave the super glue in the toolbox. Just as super glue holds on and won't let go, so some people will not let go of resentment enough to forgive. They are so inflexible that they will hold on tenaciously until the other person comes across with payment, penance or proof. Others are so stubborn they will not ask for forgiveness. No change or growth occurs until each of these people decides to let go. [5] [7]

• *Prejudice.* Lay down the one-way glasses for good. Differences in race, color, religion, culture, status, ethnic background – all these can prejudice us to refuse to forgive or be forgiven. These differences can make us more reluctant to understand the motives behind the offense and the offender. But when we look at Jesus, we see a perfect example of one who was blind to these diversities. When He spoke to the woman at the well (an immoral woman) or touched the leper (ceremonially unclean) or asked to come home with Zacchaeus (a publican), He broke through those barriers enough to love and forgive. As He said, "Do not judge, or you too will be judged. For in the same way you judge others, you will be judged, and with the measure you use, it will be measured to you" (Matthew 7:1-2).

• *A Sense of Superiority.* Discard the power suit. Forgiveness has great power, but some use it as a negative force. [6] It becomes a leveraging device to manipulate others. Lines like "I'll forgive you but you owe me" or "I'll stoop to forgive you out of the goodness of my heart" belie a sense of superiority akin to one-upmanship. We should not put the offender on a kind of "I'm-holier-than-thou" waiting period, just waiting for them to slip up. Forgiveness does not demand groveling. [7]

• *Time Frames.* There's no need to start counting days on your calendar. Forgiveness takes time. Each person has her own time frame. A well-meaning friend may encourage us to "mend our fences and forgive." While the sentiment is good and we should not prolong action unnecessarily, each person must decide when she is ready to let go of the pain and sincerely forgive. For some people, it will take considerable time to sort out their emotions. It might take more time to step back and understand why they were hurt or why they hurt someone else. Others may take a shorter route, but each follows her own timetable. [8]

What to Pack

So what should we pack for our trip? Let's make a packing list to remind us what we might need for forgiveness. This is not an inclusive list, but it will get us started.

• *Sincerity.* Sincerity is of utmost importance in giving and receiving forgiveness. Jesus stressed this after He told the parable of the unmerciful servant. He concluded by saying, "This is how my heavenly Father will treat each of you unless you forgive your brother from your heart" (Matthew 18:35). Jesus called for a genuine, heartfelt forgiveness that could not be faked or manufactured. That means that we need to be honest enough to face the offense against us but truly be willing to let it go.

• *Empathy.* Empathizing or walking in someone else's shoes can often make forgiveness easier. When we understand why someone acted as she did, we can come closer to the point of forgiving her. We should try to understand why people act as they do. Not only can it help us forgive others, but it can help us be more willing to ask for forgiveness as well. Empathy is a big step toward forgiveness because it helps us feel another's pain. [9]

• *Humility.* Author Andrew Murray stated, "Humility is not thinking less of oneself than one ought. It is not thinking of oneself at all." [10] Jesus, in the ultimate example, showed us the kind of humility it took to forgive mankind. Philippians 2:7-8 states that He "made himself nothing, taking the very nature of a servant, being made in human likeness. And being found in appearance as a man, he humbled himself and became obedient to death – even death on a cross!" It takes a servant mentality to realize that we have all sinned and are not perfect (Romans 3:23). When we are ready to pick the speck out of our brother's eye, we first need to remember the plank in our own eye (Matthew 7:3-5). Humility helps us understand that we need to be ready to forgive because in different circumstances we might have made the same mistake.

• *Commitment.* Forgiveness is not for the faint of heart. It is often like climbing two steps forward and falling a step back. It might demand more strength and energy than we thought we had. It might take years. We might find faster, easier ways to deal with our conflicts and problems – denying, overlooking, forgetting or avoiding – but these only delay what really needs to be done. Even when we think we finally accomplish forgiveness, we might find ourselves slipping back into old habits and losing ground like before. It is then that we especially need to commit ourselves to reach our destination.[11] Indian leader Mahatma Gandhi said, "The weak can never forgive. Forgiveness is the attribute of the strong." [12]

Taking Care of the Details

We are more ready for the trip than ever, but we can't leave just yet. There seem to be a hundred little details to take care of before we go. Is the light timer on? Is the mail stopped? Is the refrigerator cleaned out? How about garbage and newspapers? Has the car been checked to avoid problems on the road? Taking care of the details gives us the assurance that we have done all we can to make our trip productive.

It's the same way with the trip to forgiveness. Taking care of the details helps us avoid making unnecessary trips to the repair shop of our relationships. How many times have we said, "If only I had not … !" or "Why did I … ?" How many times have we needed to ask for forgiveness because we had breakdowns in communication, blowouts of anger, or shorts in temper?

If we know our car has been tuned up, there is less chance for a breakdown on the road. So what can we do to make our trip to forgiveness smoother?

• *Check the Oil.* A little can of oil makes a big difference in how our cars run. Likewise, the most important lubricant in our lives is love. It smoothes the rough edges of our relationships. We can put up with a lot of faults if we love someone. "Love is patient, love is kind. It does not envy, it does not boast, it is not proud" (1 Corinthians 13:4). "Be kind and compassionate to one another, forgiving each other, just as in Christ God forgave you. Be imitators of God, therefore, as dearly loved children and live a life of love, just as Christ loved us and gave himself up for us as a fragrant offering and sacrifice to God" (Ephesians 4:32-5:2).

• *Check the Pressure.* Tires maneuver better, last longer and ride smoother with the right pressure. It's the same with people. If we are under too much pressure, we are going to have a blow out – emotionally, physically or spiritually. The pressures of life can make us feel

rushed, irritable and exhausted. We should learn to slow down, cut back
on unnecessary commitments, and focus on what is important. Perhaps
then we will be less likely to blow up at someone in frustration and anger
and hence be less likely to need to ask for forgiveness!

  • *Check the Timing.* Timing is crucial to the operation of a car.
Timing is also crucial to us in our interactions with others. If we say
something inappropriate to someone at a sensitive time, it can hurt her
very deeply, so much that we might need to ask her forgiveness. On
the other hand, saying something meaningful at the right time can mean
so much to someone, whether she is grieving the loss of a loved one or
celebrating a success. "A word aptly spoken is like apples of gold in
settings of silver" (Proverbs 25:11).

A Prayer for the Journey

A friend always begins a trip with the most important thing – prayer.
When she leaves the house, she prays that the Lord will bless her with
a safe trip. When she returns, she thanks the Lord for bringing her safe-
ly home. What a wonderful habit to develop!

We could do the same thing as we begin our journey to forgiveness. For each person the names and details will be different. But we
can all pray that God will bless us on our journey and that He will give
us the qualities we need to truly forgive.

Forgiveness is an act of will. It is not automatic or accidental but rather
a choice we make.[13] God can give us the desire and power to begin. He
will help us start the trip – one step at a time. Are you ready to begin?

Stopping to Ask

1. How is each person's experience in forgiveness unique?

2. Why is forgiveness a complex process?

3. When we forgive, whom do we become more like? Why?

4. What are some qualities we need to avoid when we forgive? Why?

5. What qualities should we exemplify when we forgive? Why?

6. How do the qualities of love in 1 Corinthians 13:4-7 serve as a lubricant in our relationships?

7. How do complications of the pressures of life make us more susceptible to hurting and being hurt?

8. Why is timing important to avoid offending others?

9. Why is prayer important as we begin to forgive?

10. How is forgiveness a choice we make?

Going Further – Genesis 31

1. Why did Jacob flee from Laban with his family and herds? Why was it difficult for Jacob to confront Laban?

2. Why did Laban pursue Jacob? How did Laban draw on Jacob's empathy by mentioning his daughters and grandchildren?

3. Who stole Laban's household gods? How did she hide them from Laban?

4. How were Jacob and Laban able to resolve their differences?

5. Have you ever run away from conflict like Jacob? Was there another way to resolve your differences?

Are Some People Too Bad to Forgive?

How can we forgive someone who seems too bad to forgive? We might ask that question of a political leader in the Bible who exemplified wickedness to the next level. Manasseh, king of Judah, lived up to the meaning of his name – "causing forgetfulness."[14] Manasseh caused Judah to forget God. His crimes were many – reestablishing idolatry by erecting altars to the Baals and making Asherah poles, defiling the temple by building altars to worship the stars in both courts, practicing sorcery, witchcraft and divination, consulting mediums and spiritists, and shedding much innocent blood, including sacrificing his own sons in the fire! On an evil scale from 1-10, Manasseh was off the charts! He was so bad that he and his nation Judah were considered worse than the pagan nations they had originally been called to destroy (2 Chronicles 33:1-9).

How did God react to such iniquity? Amazingly God still cared. He called for reform, and when the people refused, He called for punishment. That is finally what got Manasseh's attention.

> So the Lord brought against them the army commanders of the king of Assyria, who took Manasseh prisoner, put a hook in his nose, bound him with bronze shackles and took him to Babylon. In his distress he sought the favor of the Lord his God and humbled himself greatly before the God of his fathers. And when he prayed to him, the Lord was moved by his entreaty and listened to his plea; so he brought him back to Jerusalem and to his kingdom. Then Manasseh knew that the Lord is God. (2 Chronicles 33:11-13)

After that experience, Manasseh threw the foreign gods and altars out of Jerusalem, restored the altar of the Lord, and commanded Judah to serve Him (2 Chronicles 33:15-16). What a transformation for someone so vile! Our just God was patient and loved Manasseh in his depravity, willing that even he should come to repentance (2 Peter 3:9). If our good God can forgive someone so bad, we certainly can too!

Chapter 3

Following the Signs

"God's love is the why of forgiveness; His Son is the how."
~Michael Youssef [1]

Even the savviest travelers get lost or, as we call it in our family, temporarily misplaced. Sometimes we are lost, and we have no idea where we are. But often we know where we are – we just don't know which way we need to go next! We need signs, landmarks, something to orient us. Then we know which direction to travel.

Imagine taking a trip to an unknown land and being directed by your own personal guide – straight from heaven! During their years of wandering in the wilderness, the Israelites probably had few signs to direct them, but they didn't need any. God led the way. There was no mistaking God's directions because they were easy to follow. By day, an enormous cloud hovered over the tabernacle when they were to set up camp. When the cloud lifted and moved, they were to break up camp and move on. By night, the cloud appeared like fire to keep them on track (Numbers 9:15-23). Though they wandered, we never learn that they were lost. God's people followed His divine signs for 40 years in the wilderness.

Signs Pointing the Way

Throughout the Old and New Testaments, God gave His people spiritual signs of His love and mercy to guide them, but they often did not read the signs very well. God provided judges and prophets to bring

His people back to Him when they had fallen away. These handpicked leaders were able to do extraordinary things to prove that they were sent from God. When Jesus came to earth, His ministry was spent demonstrating how much God really cared. Christ's work among the people proved His love and credentials. Even then the Jewish people seemed taken by surprise that a simple carpenter could do amazing things like heal the sick, cast out demons, raise the dead, and teach with an authority beyond their rabbis and scribes. In spite of all these signs and wonders, the Jewish religious leaders demanded yet another sign from heaven (Matthew 12:38; 16:1). They were so blinded by their hypocrisy and self-righteousness that they couldn't see the signs before their very eyes.

Yet the signs were there. And they are still here for us today and show the trail all the way to the cross. The Bible provides some very special signs to point us to the way of God's forgiveness. These signs guide us in the right direction and let us know we are on the right track. Our challenge is to follow those signs before us – all the way to grace and forgiveness.

Sign 1: The Lamb Slain

Lambs represent the epitome of gentleness, innocence and meekness. They would never hurt anyone. What is a more tranquil scene than a shepherd watching over his flock of sheep? Lambs were sometimes so docile and beloved that a family took one as a pet in Bible times (2 Samuel 12:3).

That is why it was such a stark contrast for God's people to see these innocent animals slaughtered on the tabernacle or temple altar. The unblemished lamb was the principal animal of sacrifice for the Jew. Deeply ingrained in the worship of every Hebrew were the vivid sights, smells and sounds of these sacrifices – the raised knives, the acrid smell of incense and smoke, the bleating cries. The Law of Moses stipulated a lamb be offered morning and evening (Numbers 28:3-4) as well as two additional lambs every Sabbath (vv. 9-10) and seven lambs each new month (v. 11). Lambs were also sacrificed on numerous other occasions: the sin offering (Leviticus 4:32), purification after childbirth (12:6), healing of a leper (14:10), the Nazirite vow (Numbers 6:14), and the redemption of the firstborn (Exodus 34:20). Sacrifices of lambs were especially important during their religious feasts: Feast of Weeks (Numbers 28:27), Feast of Trumpets (29:2), Day of Atonement (v. 8), Feast of Tabernacles (v. 13), and Passover (28:19). [2,3]

The Passover lambs had special significance to the Jews because in these symbols they remembered their flight from Egypt under the leadership of Moses. When the lamb was killed and its blood smeared on the doorpost, the angel of death would pass over that home (Exodus 12). During subsequent Passover Feasts, the priest killed the Passover Lamb by slitting its throat and collecting its blood, which was afterwards thrown on the altar. Then the lamb was handed back to the worshiper to be cooked and eaten for the Passover meal.[4]

The Greek *pascha* referred to Passover but could also mean Passover lamb. The Passover lamb was slain in the temple around noon, and Jesus was crucified at that time (John 18:28; 19:14). Paul understood the significance of this when he wrote, "For Christ, our Passover lamb, has been sacrificed" (1 Corinthians 5:7).[5]

John proclaimed, "Look, the Lamb of God, who takes away the sin of the world!" (John 1:29). Jesus was the innocent sacrifice who was willingly led to the slaughter on the cross of Calvary. He delivered us from spiritual death. He is the culmination of the entire sacrificial system. He makes any further sacrifice unnecessary (Hebrews 10).[6]

"The Lamb Slain" sign points to Jesus as our Sacrifice.

Sign 2: The Blood Shed

Blood is not a pleasant thing to us. Some people faint when they see it. But the shedding of blood was a necessary part of worship for God's people through the ages. The Mosaic Law required that blood be shed for forgiveness. Leviticus 17:11 states, "For the life of a creature is in the blood, and I have given it to you to make atonement for yourselves on the altar; it is the blood that makes atonement for one's life." The Hebrew word used for atonement is *kaphar* meaning "covering." [7] The writer of Hebrews wrote, "In fact, the law requires that nearly everything be cleansed with blood, and without the shedding of blood there is no forgiveness" (Hebrews 9:22). Forgiveness is equated with "covering." Under Mosaic Law, the blood covered their sins by the death of an innocent victim. The people believed that when they confessed their sins and blood was sprinkled on them, those very sins then belonged to the innocent animal. Being released from the penalty, they were given a new life – the life from the dead animal. It "covered" their debt. Someone else paid the debt.[8]

The animal's shed blood helps us better understand the significance of the precious blood of Jesus being shed for us. The innocent Lamb was slain so we could be covered and redeemed. The exchange or redemption was His blood for our life. Why? God loved us. John writes: "This is love: not that we loved God, but that he loved us and sent his Son as an atoning sacrifice for our sins" (1 John 4:10). And in 1 John 1:7, "But if we walk in the light, as he is in the light, we have fellowship with one another, and the blood of Jesus, his Son, purifies us from all sin." Paul echoes the concept: "Since we have now been justified by his blood, how much more shall we be saved from God's wrath through him!" (Romans 5: 9).

"The Blood Shed" sign points to Jesus as our Redeemer.

Sign 3: The Goat Sent Out

Some people do not find goats particularly attractive animals, but to the children of Israel on the Day of Atonement, they had a special significance. Leviticus 16 outlines the unusual ceremony in which Aaron (and the high priests after him) sacrificed one goat for the sins of the people. With another goat, the high priest was "to lay both hands on the head of the live goat and confess over it all the wickedness and rebellion of the Israelites – all their sins – and put them on the goat's head. He shall send the goat away into the desert in the care of a man appointed for the task. The goat will carry on itself all their sins to a solitary place; and the man shall release it in the desert" (Leviticus 16:21-22).

The scapegoat, as it was called, carried all their sins as far from the camp as possible, never to return. The Hebrew word for "forgive" is *salach*, meaning "to let go; send away." Forgiveness in Greek (*aphiemi*) has a similar meaning – "to send off or away." Both of these convey the idea of the scapegoat, a symbol of the removal of sin.[9]

With the sacrifice of the first goat, atonement was made. With the sending out of the second, guilt was removed. Jesus was our sacrifice as well as the scapegoat. He not only atoned for (covered) our sins as the sacrifice, but He bore on Himself the sins of everyone. In a sense, He became sin so we wouldn't have to bear the weight of our own sins.

He took on the guilt that we should have borne. "God made him who had no sin to be sin for us, so that in him we might become the righteousness of God" (2 Corinthians 5:21). Jesus became sin, and through Him we were cleansed to become righteousness. We traded places! He literally was our substitute. We deserved to take our punishment but He took our place instead.[10, 11] How beautifully Isaiah puts it:

> Surely he took our infirmities and carried our sorrows, yet we considered him stricken by God, smitten by him, and afflicted. But he was pierced for our transgressions, he was crushed for our iniquities; the punishment that brought us peace was upon him, and by his wounds we are healed. We all, like sheep, have gone astray, each of us has turned to his own way; and the Lord has laid on him the iniquity of us all. (Isaiah 53:4-6)

"The Goat Sent Out" sign points to Jesus as our Scapegoat.

Sign 4: The Snake Lifted Up

Few people love snakes. In fact most people are afraid of them. They slither, hiss and bite. Yet snakes played a crucial part in bringing God's people back to Him. How many times the children of Israel complained in the wilderness! God would chastise them in some way, and then Moses would pray for them. On one occasion, after hearing so much of their murmuring, God sent snakes to bite them, and many of the people died. But they repented, and Moses prayed for them. God told Moses to fashion a bronze snake on a pole. If anyone was bitten by a snake, that person could look on the bronze snake and live (Numbers 21:4-9).

Jesus compared Himself to that snake in a symbolic and literal posture in John 3:14-15: "Just as Moses lifted up the snake in the desert, so the Son of Man must be lifted up, that everyone who believes in him may have eternal life." In John 12:32 he used the same expression – "lifted up" – "But I, when I am lifted up from the earth, will draw all men to myself." The serpent, just like the cross, served as an emblem of judgment and of salvation.

Christ was lifted up on the cross and will save those who in faith look to Him and obey Him. Just like with the serpent, there is no antidote for sin and nothing else can save us from sin. "Salvation is found in no one else, for there is no other name under heaven given to men by which we must be saved" (Acts 4:12).[12]

"The Snake Lifted Up" sign points to Jesus as our Savior.

"I Am the Way"

All these signs point to Jesus as the way to forgiveness. He showed us the ultimate example of mercy and pardon in His life and death. He left us this example so we could follow in His steps (1 Peter 2:21). He told His disciples, "I am the way and the truth and the life. No one comes to the Father except through me" (John 14:6).

Christ loved people even when they were unworthy of forgiveness. "But God demonstrates his own love for us in this: While we were still sinners, Christ died for us" (Romans 5:8). Christ's loving spirit was most vividly exemplified in His words on the cross, "Father, forgive them, for they do not know what they are doing" (Luke 23:34). This was a not a request for a blanket pardon for His murderers in the depth of their sins. If it were, why would some of these same people have been told to repent and be baptized in Acts 2:38? Rather Jesus demonstrated a forgiving attitude in asking God to allow them an opportunity to be forgiven. We need to strive for this loving, forgiving attitude toward everyone.[13]

Jesus had the power to call for reinforcements to retaliate against those who arrested and killed Him. He told Peter, "Do you think I cannot call on my Father, and he will at once put at my disposal more than twelve legions of angels?" (Matthew 26:53). Yet the Lord chose to suffer and die for us. He chose love over revenge. Sadly, some people think retaliation is the only response to injury. Chapter 4 deals with what happens when people choose this.

Stopping to Ask

1. What did the expression "written code" refer to in Colossians 2:13-14? What financial document is it compared to today?

2. Why could writing be wiped clean on documents during New Testament times?

3. On what occasions did the Law of Moses stipulate that lambs be sacrificed?

4. Why did the Passover lamb have special significance to Jews?

5. What meanings did the Greek word *pascha* have? What connection did Paul make between Christ and the Passover lamb in 1 Corinthians 5:7?

6. Why was it important to kill a creature for atonement?

7. What was the Hebrew word meaning "covering"? What implication did it have with atonement and blood?

8. How did the ceremony on the Day of Atonement involve two goats? How is Christ like both goats?

9. What are the Greek and Hebrew words meaning "forgive"? How do they convey the meaning of the scapegoat?

10. How is Jesus like the snake lifted up in the wilderness (John 3:14-15; 12:32)?

Going Further –
John 19:19-22; Matthew 27:37-38

1. What did the sign say that Pilate had the soldiers post above Jesus on the cross? What was the purpose of the sign?

2. Why were the Romans particularly suspicious of anyone who claimed to be king? Why did the chief priests want the wording changed?

3. Was Jesus guilty of the crime stated on the sign? Was Jesus guilty of any crime?

4. If the men crucified with Jesus had signs posted on their crosses, what would they have read? If we each had suffered on a cross as we deserved, what would the signs stating our crimes say?

What Does God Do With Our Sins?

Although we as Christians see the tangible effects that sin and forgiveness can have, we often have a difficult time understanding the real significance of each one. We can't fully fathom how deplorable sin is, and we cannot understand fully how much God hates it. Similarly, we cannot really appreciate how great a gift forgiveness is. One day we hope to understand, but for now we muddle along with our finiteness. We can only try to get into our heads the wonder of God's grace and our inadequacy ever to receive it.

God has given us some images in His Word that help better flesh out these concepts. These images give heavenly concepts an earthly handle so we can understand them better. The specific ones below show us in human terms what God figuratively does with our sins when He forgives us. They demonstrate how far God will go to get rid of them.

" 'Come now, let us reason together,' says the Lord. 'Though your sins are like scarlet, they shall be as white as snow; though they are red as crimson, they shall be like wool' " (Isaiah 1:18).

"I, even I, am he who blots out your transgressions, for my own sake, and remembers your sins no more"(Isaiah 43:25).

"I have swept away your offenses like a cloud, your sins like the morning mist. Return to me, for I have redeemed you" (Isaiah 44:22).

"In your love you kept me from the pit of destruction; you have put all my sins behind your back" (Isaiah 38:17b).

"For as high as the heavens are above the earth, so great is his love for those who fear him; as far as the east is from the west, so far has he removed our transgressions from us" (Psalm 103:11-12).

"Who is a God like you, who pardons sin and forgives the transgression of the remnant of his inheritance? You do not stay angry forever but delight to show mercy. You will again have compassion on us; you will tread our sins underfoot and hurl all our iniquities into the depths of the sea" (Micah 7:18-19).

As Holocaust survivor Corrie ten Boom said, after God hurls our sins into the depths of the ocean, He sticks up a sign that reads, "NO FISHING ALLOWED!"[14]

Chapter 4

Beyond Road Rage

"Whoever opts for revenge should dig two graves."
~ Chinese Proverb[1]

Once a Sunday school teacher noticed two little boys arguing in the back of the class. On further investigation, she discovered that one had hit the other before class. Seeing this as a golden opportunity to show forgiveness in action, she called the boys to the front and emphasized how God wants us to forgive everyone. Then came the moment of truth.

"Jeremy, will you forgive Nathan?"

"Sure," Jeremy answered, at which point he proceeded to punch Nathan in the stomach.

"Hey, what are you doing, Jeremy?" the flustered teacher cried as she pulled the boys apart.

"Oh, I'll forgive him but I had to get back at him first!"[2]

Just like those little boys, when someone hurts us, our natural inclination is to get even. Think about when …

… someone cuts you off in traffic.

… a coworker backstabs you.

… a church member embarrasses you at a fellowship.

Though these offenses differ in degree, one thing remains – our knee-jerk reaction is not to forgive. Road rage is not confined just to the highway! It is difficult to be kind and forgive someone who causes pain to us or those we love. After all, they hurt us. Aren't we justified in hurting them back? Isn't revenge supposed to be sweet?

Revenge might seem momentarily sweet. But in the end it is ultimately bitter and tragic. We see revenge on the late-breaking news in road rage, gang shootings and terrorist violence. Yet it is nothing new. Retaliation was a common way to settle accounts in the ancient world. Its roots go back to the first family in the Bible.

Early Roots of Revenge

Adam and Eve's son Cain maliciously killed his brother Abel. Because of this sin, Cain was driven out of the Lord's presence to become a restless wanderer who worked the ground with little to show for his efforts. Cain must have been afraid of revenge even back then because he complained that whoever found him would kill him for the treacherous act of killing his brother. "But the Lord said to him, 'Not so; if anyone kills Cain, he will suffer vengeance seven times over.' Then the Lord put a mark on Cain so that no one who found him would kill him" (Genesis 4:15).

Revenge – inflicting injury for injury or avenging oneself or another – was common in the Old Testament. In the name of vengeance, families were torn apart by murder and hate. They tried to settle the score, but retaliation often led to more violence.

Remember the famous Hatfield-McCoy feud, the story of folklore and songs? It really did happen, although many people are not certain what started it. We know that, before they came to terms, 27 family members had died.[3] Many years before, another family feud in the Bible started between two clans with similarly disastrous results.

The Fruits of Vengeance

Her brothers were understandably outraged. The prince of the land had raped their only sister. One brother would be bad enough for the prince to deal with, but a whole family of brothers were waiting to unleash their fury. The clan mentality of this primitive culture was taking over. They wanted revenge!

How could they measure out justice for what the prince Shechem had done, even if he did want to marry their sister Dinah? They decided to formulate a plan. They demanded that Shechem, his father Hamor, and all the townsmen be circumcised. Then on the third day, when they would still be in pain, Dinah's full-blood brothers Simeon and Levi retaliated with full force. They attacked the unsuspecting city, killing every male, carrying off their women and children, and looting their belongings. Revenge left a bloody and deadly path (Genesis 34:25-29).

Jacob, ashamed of his sons' conduct, was afraid of severe reprisals from the inhabitants of the land. He decided to pack up and leave the area. "Then Jacob said to Simeon and Levi, 'You have brought trouble on me by making me a stench to the Canaanites and Perizzites, the people living in this land. We are few in number, and if they join forces against me and attack me, I and my household will be destroyed" (Genesis 34:30). Simeon and Levi tried to justify their actions, but taking matters into their own hands only made things worse.[4] Generations later, others would follow the same course.

Vengeful David?

As a young soldier, David had opportunities to retaliate, but he refrained. When King Saul sought to kill him, David had two chances to kill Saul but refused (1 Samuel 24:5-7; 25:33; 26:9-11). The young warrior knew that God would avenge him in His own time.

During this time David came closest to modern road rage in his dealings with Nabal. David, riding angry with 400 armed men, was ready to pay Nabal back for his lack of hospitality. "David had just said, 'It's been useless – all my watching over this fellow's property in the desert so that nothing of his was missing. He paid me back evil for good. May God deal with David, be it ever so severely, if by morning I leave alive one male of all who belong to him!'" (1 Samuel 25:21-22). David later admitted that the quick thinking of Abigail not only saved her household from tragedy, but also saved him from having "on his conscience the staggering burden of needless bloodshed or of having avenged himself" (v. 31).

But even the man after God's own heart was not above revenge. In his later life, forgiveness without retaliation did not come so easily. At one of the lowest times of his life, David was fleeing Jerusalem to escape Absalom and his rebellious army. Shimei, a relative of Saul's, showered David with dirt and pelted him and his officials with stones.

"As he cursed, Shimei said, 'Get out, get out, you man of blood, you scoundrel! The Lord has repaid you for all the blood you shed in the household of Saul, in whose place you have reigned. The Lord has handed the kingdom over to your son Absalom. You have come to ruin because you are a man of blood!' " (2 Samuel 16:7-8). Abishai, a soldier of David's, asked to cut off Shimei's head, but David said to leave him alone. David thought the Lord had told Shimei to treat David that way and perhaps God would repay the king with good for the cursing he received that day.

When David was triumphant after Absalom's death, Shimei and a thousand Benjamites rushed to the Jordan River to help the king however they could. We don't know if Shimei's motives were sincere or if he only intended to save his head! Whatever his reason, Shimei fell prostrate before David and begged his forgiveness. Abishai again asked David if he could kill Shimei and again David refused. David promised Shimei on oath that he would not kill him (2 Samuel 19:15-23).

But sadly the story didn't end there. Apparently David never forgot the verbal and physical abuse he endured. Speaking of Shimei on his deathbed, he reminded Solomon, "Bring his gray head down to the grave in blood" (1 Kings 2:9). How would you like for those to be your last recorded words? Later working circumstances to his advantage, Solomon had Shimei killed (2:36-46).

The Vengeance Goes On

Shimei was not the only one with a death warrant from David's deathbed. David also requested that Solomon kill Joab as well. Joab was David's nephew and longtime army commander. Joab had not only plotted and killed Abner, Saul's army commander (2 Samuel 3:22-39), but also Amasa, Absalom's commander and another nephew of David's (20:4-13). In cloak-and-dagger style, Joab had murdered these key leaders at a time when David was trying to reconcile the kingdom. Could it be that Joab's reasons were not totally out of loyalty to David? Scripture tells us that Joab murdered Abner because Abner had killed Joab's brother Ashahel years before (2:22-23). Joab might have feared Amasa's loyalty to Absalom, but Amasa had been given Joab's long held job as army commander (17:25). No wonder Joab felt justified in getting revenge!

But the revenge didn't stop! Could David have actually wanted retaliation against Joab for killing his son Absalom as he hung by his long hair from a tree? David had asked that no one harm Absalom, but Joab felt it more important to kill the rebellious leader (2 Samuel 18:9-15). Or had David lost trust in Joab after he supported Adonijah in his bid to usurp the throne from Solomon (1 Kings 1:7)? Perhaps for all these reasons, Solomon had Joab killed in the tabernacle where he had fled for refuge (1 Kings 2:28-33).[5]

We can see from these examples that vengeance begets more vengeance. If unchecked, the tragic consequences go on for generations. Unless measures are taken, the one-upmanship of revenge often never becomes resolved. But retaliation never solves the problem; it only adds to it. Referring to the inhibited course of vengeance, theologian Lewis Smedes writes: "It ties both the injured and the injurer to an escalator of pain. Both are stuck on the escalator as long as parity is demanded, and the escalator never stops, never lets anyone off." [6]

Seeing Eye to Eye on Righting Wrongs

To curb the violence of the vendetta, the Lord provided the "tit for tat" law or the Lex Talionis for His people. This law was otherwise known as an "eye for an eye" or a "tooth for a tooth" (Exodus 21:23-25; Leviticus 24:19-20; Deuteronomy 19:21).[7] Not only was it in the Law of Moses but also in earlier law codes such as the Code of Hammurabi and Middle Assyrian Laws.[8] At first glance, it looks savage and merciless, but in reality it limited vengeance. Just like Simeon and Levi's retaliation, the vendetta and tribal feuding was a characteristic way of dealing with injury and damage in their primitive society. This law was the beginning of mercy.[9]

The Lex Talionis was never meant to give a person the right to take affairs into his own hands. Rather he was to work through a judge who determined the punishment according to the crime (Deuteronomy 19:18-19). The law could almost never be taken literally because one good eye might be knocked out and a bad eye taken in replacement. Similarly one decaying tooth might be knocked out and a healthy one knocked out to take its place.[10] While during the time of Jesus a party of the Sadducees still applied the letter of this law, most Pharisees in-

sisted on financial settlements with specific money values assessed.[11]
If someone injured another, he was liable for pain, injury, healing, in-
dignity suffered and loss of time. Some of these compensations sound
strangely familiar to our courts today![12]

There was a definite place for mercy in Old Testament Law (Leviticus
19:18; Proverbs 24:29; 25:21-22; Lamentations 3:30).[13] God provided
cities of refuge, where someone who had unintentionally murdered
someone could run for protection (Numbers 35:6-34). An "avenger of
blood" or relative of the murder victim was given the liberty to kill a
murderer on sight if the murder was committed intentionally (Genesis
9:5; Numbers 35:19). But if someone accidentally killed another, he
was to flee to one of the six cities of refuge and appear before the as-
sembly to be judged. If found innocent, he remained there until the death
of the high priest. Then he could return to his hometown (Joshua 20).[14]

It was actually up to the wronged individual whether he or she wanted to prosecute or not. But often mercy and forgiveness were not what
those who had been wronged desired. If they could not take it into their
own hands, they wanted revenge to the letter of the law. The problem
with the Lex Talionis was that often instead of limiting vengeance, it
justified vindictiveness. There had to be a better way, even if it meant
going beyond what was expected.

Stopping to Ask

1. Why did Cain complain about what might happen to him (Genesis
   4:14-15)? Which descendant of Cain felt he would also be avenged
   for killing a man (v. 24)?

2. How did Dinah's brothers avenge her rape by Shechem? What pre-
   caution did Jacob take to avoid more retaliation? How did Jacob
   later describe Simeon and Levi (Genesis 49:5-7)?

3. What did the Law of Moses command about seeking revenge and
   bearing a grudge (Leviticus 19:17-18)?

4. Who prevented David from avenging Nabal? How did she soothe
   his anger? What later happened between them after Nabal died?

5. What did Shimei do to David as he was leaving Jerusalem? How did David eventually retaliate?

6. Whom did Joab murder in cloak-and-dagger style? What might have been Joab's reasons to murder these army leaders?

7. Why might David have asked Solomon to have Joab killed? Which son of David's did Joab kill?

8. What was the Lex Talionis? If used properly, how could it limit vengeance?

9. How do Proverbs 24:29; 25:21-22; and Lamentations 3:30 show that mercy was to be practiced in Old Testament Law?

10. What were the cities of refuge? What was their purpose (Joshua 20)?

Going Further – Judges 19:16–20:48

1. Who did the old man offer the wicked men of Gibeah in Benjamin? Who did the Levite give them? What sin did the men commit?

2. Why did the Levite dismember his concubine into 12 parts and send them into each region of Israel?

3. Why did the Israelites meet in Mizpah? What was the decided verdict? How did they allow for only those guilty to be punished, and what did the Benjamites decide to do instead?

4. How did the need for justice escalate into full-scale war between the Benjamites and the rest of the tribes of Israel? What can we do to prevent the escalation of retaliation between people?

Why Did Jesus Assert His Authority to Forgive Sins?

Jesus was the Lord of the unexpected. He often caught people off guard. Healing the paralyzed man was no exception. One day Jesus was in a house so crowded there was no room for anyone else. All of a sudden everyone looked up, and the roof was being torn away by four men who lowered their friend on a mat right in front of Jesus. That was unexpected enough. But then, instead of healing him, Jesus pronounced that his sins were forgiven. That was totally unexpected!

The Pharisees and teachers of the law were wondering how Jesus could claim to do such a thing. They considered it blasphemy. They understood that only God could forgive sins. However, they refused to acknowledge the obvious: Jesus was God. Amazing miracles, unexplainable healings, authoritative teaching like no other rabbi – all these failed to convince them that Jesus, the Son of Man, was in fact divine. That God could also become man was totally unexpected!

Christ knew what the Pharisees and teachers of the law were thinking. Instead of answering questions, He asked: " 'Why are you thinking these things in your hearts? Which is easier: to say, "Your sins are forgiven," or to say, "Get up and walk"? But that you may know that the Son of Man has authority on earth to forgive sins.' He said to the paralyzed man, 'I tell you, get up, take your mat and go home' " (Luke 5:22-24). Jesus was saying that if He had the power to heal, He certainly had the power to forgive sins. Only God could give such power. And to prove He had that power, He healed the man. One action – healing – substantiated the other – forgiveness. Both were declarations of Christ's divinity.

A common belief among the Jews was that all sickness came from sin (John 9:2) and that a sick man did not recover until his sins were forgiven. So according to their own belief, the man's sins were forgiven![15] The proof was hard to deny – the man who was borne on the mat was now carrying it and praising God. The crowd in the house also praised God and talked about the remarkable things they had seen. But with the Son of God among them, what did they expect?

Chapter 5

Going Beyond the Expected

"The children of heaven bleed grace when cut by others,
and they receive a transfusion of grace in the process!"
~ John Ensor [1]

Hitchhiking in America is a lost art. In years past, it was not unusual to see someone "thumbin' " a ride to get from point "A" to point "B." But fear of strangers and violence has curtailed hitchhiking to very few "thumbers" and even fewer "takers."

In ancient times, the Roman soldier didn't have the luxury of hitchhiking. He was expected to walk or march to his destination with his gear on his back. There was no hitchin' a ride for the Roman legion.

The Roman soldier, however, did know about the next best thing to hitchhiking. If he saw an able-bodied subject of the empire, he had the right to commandeer the unfortunate soul to carry his load. This was not a small stash of his extra clothes but rather a full pack of possibly 60 pounds of tools, weapons and rations.[2] Not only would the victim be laden with a heavy load, but he would also be bearing it for a despised conqueror. It was a doubly distasteful task, and the Jews angrily and unwillingly complied. The Romans, after all, were hated for their treatment of God's people. Some Jewish sects, like the Zealots, even sought to retaliate and overthrow these enemies with force. There was no room for good will or forgiveness – period!

This setting provoked Jesus to tell His followers to go beyond what was expected – to go the second mile with anyone who forced them. A Roman mile was 1,000 paces, less than a mile today, but still quite

an excursion with a 60-pound pack on your back![3] That would add up
to a total of 4,000 paces if you walked back to where you started.

A Better Way

Going the second mile was not the only challenge Jesus had for His
listeners. Throughout the Sermon on the Mount, Jesus contrasted the
Jews' traditions and interpretation of the Old Law with His radical new
law. In Matthew 5:38-42, He focused specifically on the Jews' manip-
ulation of "an eye for an eye" for their own purpose of revenge. Christ
told the crowd:

> You have heard that it was said, "Eye for eye, and tooth for
> tooth." But I tell you, Do not resist an evil person. If some-
> one strikes you on the right cheek, turn to him the other also.
> And if someone wants to sue you and take your tunic, let
> him have your cloak as well. If someone forces you to go
> one mile, go with him two miles. Give to the one who asks
> you, and do not turn away from the one who wants to bor-
> row from you.

In this passage, Jesus calls for a generous, forgiving heart with no
retaliation,

• even if you are insulted.
• even if you are sued for necessities.
• even if you are forced to carry a heavy and inconvenient load.
• even if someone asks to borrow something.

A closer look at these teachings show us how radical they were. Being
struck on the right cheek was considered the most grievous insult, pros-
ecuted by Jewish as well as Roman courts. This insult was delivered
by the back of the hand, which was considered twice as insulting as
the front of the hand. Jesus said to be ready to turn your cheek for another injury and insult.[4]

You could give your inner tunic as a pledge or legal fine because
even a poor man might have a change of tunic. But you were not obligated to give up your more valuable outer cloak because it could serve
as a blanket at night (Exodus 22:26-27; Deuteronomy 24:12-13).[5] Jesus
said to be willing to give up your cloak anyway.

Instead of going one mile, Jesus said to go two. When someone asks

to borrow something, Jesus said be willing to share with whoever asks.
These actions exceeded what was expected. Instead of demanding
restitution for these personal affronts, a Christian should be ready to
go further and give more.[6]

Jesus' Alternative

Jesus then gave an alternative to "love your neighbor and hate your
enemy." This maxim had served as the accepted Jewish standard.[7] No
Old Testament scripture taught Jews to hate an enemy, although some
scriptures were taken to mean that (Deuteronomy 23:3-6; 25:17-19;
Psalms 109; 137:7-9; 139:19-22).[8] In fact, the Old Law taught caring
about the needs of enemies (Exodus 23:4-5; 1 Samuel 24:19; Proverbs
25:21-22).[9] Although Leviticus 19:18 taught God's people to love their
neighbor, some Jews further deduced that they should hate their enemy.[10] Jesus told them instead, "Love your enemies and pray for those
who persecute you" (Matthew 5:44).

The word for "love" here is the Greek *agape*, meaning "unconquer-
able benevolence, invincible goodwill." [11] This is a love not of the heart
but the will. It is a love that holds no bitterness or revenge. It prays for
an enemy. It is very difficult to pray for someone you hate! [12]

Love your enemies – what a contrast! Only in this spirit of love and
grace in the face of opposition can forgiveness flourish. Love is the
underlying motive for going beyond the expected and going further to
forgiveness. Jesus directed His listeners and us to a higher plane in personal relations. In love, the world finds a far better way of treating others. But how do we put this love into practice? How did Jesus act when
He was slapped, a gesture considered to be a grave insult in that culture?

During His trial, Jesus was accused of blasphemy by Caiaphas, the
high priest. The teachers of the law and the elders began to attack Jesus.
"Then they spit in his face and struck him with their fists. Others slapped
him and said, 'Prophesy to us, Christ. Who hit you?' " (Matthew 26:67-
68). Matthew does not record Jesus' reaction, but we can see a fulfillment of the prophecy of Christ's suffering in Isaiah 50:6: "I offered my
back to those who beat me, my cheeks to those who pulled out my
beard; I did not hide my face from mocking and spitting." In parallel
passages in the Gospels, Jesus was mocked, beaten, blindfolded, flogged

and struck in the face at various times during His trial (Mark 14:63-65; Luke 22:63-65; John 19:1-3).

In John's account, Jesus answered the high priest during His trial about teaching openly in the synagogues or in the temple. Note that, even in His defense, He did not retaliate. "When Jesus said this, one of the officials nearby struck him in the face. 'Is this the way you answer the high priest?' he demanded. 'If I said something wrong,' Jesus replied, 'testify as to what is wrong. But if I spoke the truth, why did you strike me?' " (John 18:22-23).

By telling us to turn the other cheek, the Lord was not justifying physical or verbal abuse. Neither was He prohibiting defending Himself or someone else. He stood up for Himself in the previous scripture. Rather, He is urging us to be prepared for more than one insult. In doing so, we follow His example: "When they hurled their insults at him, he did not retaliate; when he suffered, he made no threats. Instead, he entrusted himself to him who judges justly" (1 Peter 2:23).

In Romans 12:17-21, Paul underscores Christ's teaching of replacing retaliation with love:

> Do not repay anyone evil for evil. Be careful to do what is right in the eyes of everybody. If it is possible, as far as it depends on you, live at peace with everyone. Do not take revenge, my friends, but leave room for God's wrath, for it is written: "It is mine to avenge; I will repay," says the Lord. On the contrary: "If your enemy is hungry, feed him; if he is thirsty, give him something to drink. In doing this, you will heap burning coals on his head." Do not be overcome by evil, but overcome evil with good.

Paul quoted Proverbs 25:21-22 and might have thought that the burning coals represented the raging guilt and shame that the sinner feels. Or he may have intended it as a reference to eternal punishment with burning coals representing the fires of hell.[13] Whatever his original meaning, Paul stressed that we should not retaliate because the Lord will even the score someday. God, the great judge, will not be too harsh or too lenient.[14] Only by allowing God's love to flow through us can we overcome evil with good. Only then can we go beyond the expected and refuse to retaliate when we are hurt. Booker T. Washington wisely said, "I will not allow any man to make me lower myself by hating him." Bible commentator William Barclay added, "The only real way to destroy an enemy is to make him a friend." [15]

All the Advantages?

With all this going-the-second-mile, loving-your-enemy attitude, it might seem that oppressors and abusers get all the advantages. Are Christians getting a raw deal? After all, they are not to retaliate against their oppressors. After getting hurt, they are to love and forgive their enemies. It seems the score is overwhelmingly in favor of the wicked. Is the one who forgives and does not retaliate always the loser?

Take Marietta Jaeger, for example. In June 1973 she, her husband Bill, and their five children set off from Detroit for a camping trip out West. One night at Three Forks, Mont., a man cut the canvas of their tent and kidnapped 7-year-old Susie. Every parents' nightmare became a reality for the Jaegers.

As days of searching turned into weeks, Marietta became so angry with the kidnapper she told her husband that even if her daughter were returned, she would kill the kidnapper with her bare hands. But then she remembered what she had been taught in childhood – to love her enemies and pray for them. Although nothing changed in the search for her child, she began to consider an alternative to revenge. Meanwhile, her husband silently brooded and carried a gun wherever he went.

Marietta made a concerted, though mechanical, effort to try to see the kidnapper as a member of the human race who had intrinsic worth. She resolved not to talk about the criminal in subhuman terms. She tried to wish that something good would happen to him.

Marietta didn't know it, but she had been preparing for the phone call she received a year after her daughter was abducted. In the middle of the night she received a call from the kidnapper. Marietta calmly talked with him for more than an hour. Police were able to match his voiceprint and arrested a suspect. Soon after arrest, he confessed to not only murdering Susie but also another girl and two boys. Marietta's calm, forgiving attitude almost certainly saved lives. The kidnapper committed suicide soon after capture.

Bill Jaeger's rage over this injustice never subsided. As he seethed over their agonizing loss, he developed heart problems and bleeding ulcers. At 56 he collapsed, dead from a heart attack.

Marietta, meanwhile, has slowly learned to give up the rancor of bitterness. She knows from experience that forgiveness takes diligent, daily discipline.[16] She tells others, "If anyone thinks forgiveness is for wimps, they haven't tried it. ... If you remain vindictive, you give the offender another victim. Anger, hatred, and resentment would have taken my life as surely as Susie's life was taken."[17]

Breaking the Cycle

The choice is ours. We can do what the world expects or, as Christians, we can go beyond the expected. We can choose anger, hatred and retaliation or love, grace and forgiveness. Which will it be? Author Margaret Hebblethwaite aptly writes,

> True Christian forgiveness is a way of showing just how appalling sin is, because the ultimate message of forgiveness is this: What you have done is so terrible that nothing like that must ever be allowed to happen again on this earth. Every fiber of my being and every ounce of my energy must be turned to fighting this evil. To put a stop to such things happening I will break the cycle. Instead of repaying injury with injury, hurt with hurt, I will put a spoke in the wheel of revenge and stop it dead in its path. The cycle is broken.[18]

Stopping to Ask

1. In Luke 6:27-31, what basic ideas does Jesus ask of His followers? What verse is the theme that runs throughout?

2. What was Jesus' alternative to an "eye for eye and tooth for tooth"?

3. What was the traditional Jewish maxim for treating others? What was Jesus' alternative?

4. How did Jesus react when He was slapped during His trial (Matthew 26:67-68; John 18:22-23)? What did a slap with the back of the hand mean?

5. When Jesus told us to "turn the other cheek," was He justifying verbal or physical abuse?

6. Who was forced to carry Jesus' cross (Luke 23:26)?

7. Which prophet was slapped in 1 Kings 22:24? Who slapped him?

8. What attitudes toward enemies are depicted in these scriptures: Deuteronomy 23:3-6; 25:17-19; Psalms 109; 137:7-9; 139:21-22? How are personal enemies to be treated (Exodus 23:4-5; 1 Samuel 24:19; Proverbs 25:21)? How were individual non-Israelites to be treated (Leviticus 19:34; Deuteronomy 10:19)?

9. What Old Testament scripture did Paul quote in Romans 12:20? What possible significance did coals of fire on someone's head have?

10. How does forgiveness break the cycle of revenge?

Going Further – 2 Kings 7:3-16

1. During the famine in Samaria, what did the four lepers at the gate decide to do? Why did they decide to take such a dangerous risk?

2. What did they find in the Aramean camp? What had the Lord done there? Why do you think the lepers hid their plunder?

3. Why did they decide to share their good news? Given the indignities that lepers suffered at that time, why was their generosity going beyond what was expected?

4. What are some examples you have seen of people who have gone beyond the expected, even in difficult circumstances?

Did Jesus Give the Apostles the Power to Forgive Sins?

When Jesus appeared to His disciples in the upper room the Sunday evening of His resurrection day, He revealed more than the nail prints in His hands or His ability to move through locked doors. He also revealed the connection between the Holy Spirit and the Great Commission in preaching the forgiveness of sins. John 20:21-23 states, "Again Jesus said, 'Peace be with you! As the Father has sent me, I am sending you.' And with that he breathed on them and said, 'Receive the Holy Spirit. If you forgive anyone his sins, they are forgiven; if you do not forgive them, they are not forgiven.' "

The fulfillment of Jesus' words were dramatically initiated in the apostles' sermon on Pentecost. On that occasion they were filled with the Holy Spirit (Acts 2:4). The exceptional measure of the Spirit they received empowered them to proclaim the conditions of forgiveness to the Jews there, many of whom had clamored for the crucifixion of the Lord. The apostles proclaimed to their listeners as Peter did: "Repent and be baptized, every one of you, in the name of Jesus Christ for the forgiveness of your sins. And you will receive the gift of the Holy Spirit" (v. 38).[19]

On Pentecost the apostles first preached the forgiveness that God had already made possible through Christ's death and resurrection. The literal meaning of the Greek in John 20:23 is, "Those whose sins you forgive have already been forgiven; those whose sins you do not forgive have not been forgiven." [20] The apostles declared the terms by which one might receive salvation from sins – repentance and baptism – but God had already provided that salvation through the gospel.

God's forgiveness to people did not hinge on whether Peter or another apostle forgave them. It depended on their faith and obedience to the gospel plan. The same is true today. No human on earth has the authority to forgive or absolve sins. Only Jesus had that power on earth (Mark 2:5-12).[21] The apostles, through the Holy Spirit, proclaimed the full message of forgiveness, and that was where the power lay. And that is where the power still is – in the inspired, God-breathed message of the gospel (Romans 1:16).

Part Two:

Getting Around the Obstacles

D riving on an interstate highway is one of the supreme tests of physical agility, mental alertness, and plain old daring-do chutzpa. You take your life into your own hands as you dodge construction barrels, claustrophobic side barriers and highway flaggers. As if these obstacles were not enough, you must have eyes on all sides of your head to miss certain speed-demon drivers weaving in and out of traffic and leaving havoc in their path. Only the strong will arrive at their destination. Like fish, you either go with the flow or get swallowed by the bigger fish.

But country roads have their own brand of obstacles – whether it is the turtle-like tractor pulling a wagon-load of hay, the casual motorist out for a Sunday drive with no place in particular to go, or a bridge washed out by high creek water.

Wherever we travel, things can get in our way.

Our journey to forgiveness is that way. Our plans and intentions can be good, but preconceived ideas and personal feelings can get in our path. We can lose our way and start going in circles, only to get directions that don't help us that much. We can get overburdened by excess baggage and frustrated by potholes much bigger than we imagined. Part 2 will look at some obstacles that can slow down our trip and mire us in the mud of fear or inaction.

Chapter 6

You Can't Get There From Here

*"Those who cannot forgive others break the
bridge over which they themselves must pass."*
~ Confucius [1]

A fter driving around the countryside and getting hopelessly lost, a lady stopped to ask a farmer for directions. After some slow deliberation, he mused, "Well, you could turn right when you get to the Stewart farm ... no, you better pass the general store and take a left ... no, that won't work either." Finally, he scratched his head, saying, "Lady, you can't get there from here!"

The same is true about receiving forgiveness. We can't get there from here – if we don't forgive others. We cannot receive forgiveness from God if we do not offer it to others.

English evangelist John Wesley realized this principle when he came to America in the 1700s as a missionary. When Wesley discussed a troublemaker with the governor of the colony of Georgia, James Oglethorpe, Oglethorpe resolutely stated, "I never forgive."

Wesley replied, "Then, sir, I hope you never sin." [2]

In His model prayer, Jesus said we should pray to be forgiven by God as we have also forgiven our debtors (Matthew 6:12). He added, "For if you forgive men when they sin against you, your heavenly Father will also forgive you. But if you do not forgive men their sins, your Father will not forgive your sins" (vv. 14-15). God's mercy will be extended as far for us as we have extended it to others (5:7).

Jesus does not give us a choice concerning forgiveness. Remember that initially in the parable of the unmerciful servant the king freely forgave his servant his exorbitant debt. When the first servant was unwilling to forgive his fellow servant, the king turned over the guilty servant "to the jailers to be tortured, until he should pay back all he owed" (Matthew 18:34). We shudder to think of such a ruthless monarch. Isn't this a far cry from our merciful God? Yet, Jesus pointedly exclaimed, "This is how my heavenly Father will treat each of you unless you forgive your brother from your heart" (v. 35). There is no mistaking His message. Our God of mercy is also a God of justice. We must learn to forgive!

Taking a Good Look at Ourselves

How can we begin to forgive someone else when it seems impossible? Perhaps we should begin by looking at ourselves. We have done bad things that call for God and others to forgive us. We have been thoughtless, proud, selfish – the list goes on. That's the idea that Lewis Smedes had when he wrote: "Our own faults, therefore, reduce the gap between us and whoever did us wrong. We do not toss our forgiving down from the peak of a holy mountain; we are in the valley with those who hurt us." [3] We are not above the sins of others. If circumstances had been reversed, we might have done as they did – or even worse! [4]

That is just what the teachers and Pharisees discovered when they brought in the woman caught in adultery. By asking Jesus whether they should stone her as Moses commanded, they intended to entrap the Lord. Instead they trapped themselves! Non-threateningly, Jesus wrote on the ground with His finger. "When they kept on questioning him, he straightened up and said to them, 'If any one of you is without sin, let him be the first to throw a stone at her.' Again he stooped down and wrote on the ground" (John 8:7-8).

Recognition of past offenses slowly dawned on each listener, from the older ones down. Each saw himself as the sinner he was. As each man slipped away, soon no one was left to condemn her. Jesus told her, "Go now and leave your life of sin" (John 8:11b).

Here Jesus exemplified what He taught about critically judging others: "Do not judge, and you will not be judged. Do not condemn, and you will not be condemned. Forgive, and you will be forgiven" (Luke

6:37). He showed us that our attitude is the key to judging and forgiving others and demonstrated that only in forgiving would we be forgiven.

It would be nice to think that the adulterous woman did not sin any more after that, but we know better. We know we all sin and will keep sinning, even with the best of intentions to do otherwise (Romans 3:23). Perhaps John was thinking about this when he wrote, "My dear children, I write this to you so that you will not sin. But if anybody does sin, we have one who speaks to the Father in our defense – Jesus Christ, the Righteous One. He is the atoning sacrifice for our sins, and not only for ours but also for the sins of the whole world" (1 John 2:1-2).

Because we all make mistakes, we should allow for each other's faults. We should extend grace to each other as God's grace has been extended to us. As Paul encouraged the Colossians, "Therefore, as God's chosen people, holy and dearly loved, clothe yourselves with compassion, kindness, humility, gentleness and patience. Bear with each other and forgive whatever grievances you may have against one another. Forgive as the Lord forgave you. And over all these virtues put on love, which binds them all together in perfect unity" (Colossians 3:12-14).

Looking Through God's Eyes

When we forgive people, we should try to see them through God's eyes.[5] We should strive to see them as people of incomparable worth, as valued members of the human race. Because they are God's creation, they deserve respect, no matter what they have done. We should also see them as people, just like us, who make mistakes. When we understand that, we come closer to developing empathy for them.[6]

People have reasons for the things they do. Though their reasons might not be justified, we can still try to understand. Developing an understanding of people can make forgiving them easier, even if we don't condone or excuse their actions.[7] Jesus could look beyond the shame of the adulterous woman and really see and understand her. We should strive to develop this empathy or genuine understanding for others, especially for someone we want to forgive. This empathy, with time, can generate a feeling of compassion, which in turn can lead to forgiveness.[8] It has been said, "Empathy is the plow that breaks up the hard ground of our hearts."[9]

Empathy's immense power to move enemies toward forgiveness was demonstrated in a conference among warring factions in Liberia in 1980. A violent military coup in this African country had erupted with unprecedented brutality. The conference of about 500 representatives from antagonistic tribal and governmental groups could have ended with nothing accomplished. But something happened to change the course of the meeting. The participants in the conference broke into groups of three and shared their tragic stories. They related how children watched their parents being executed. Women were raped. Mothers saw their sons taken away. Many wept as they listened to each other's stories. In sharing each heartache, they began to develop empathy for one another. They began to understand that even their enemies were human and had suffered losses like themselves. They realized their shared suffering was more important than their differences.[10]

It seems incredible that these sworn enemies could find a common ground but they did. How about us? Can we find within ourselves empathy for those who have mistreated and hurt us? How can empathy make the way to forgiveness easier?

Steps to Empathy

Everett Worthington in his book *Five Steps to Forgiveness* writes, "A general understanding of people takes us only to the threshold of empathy. To empathize, we must discern why *this person* has hurt *me* in this way." [11] He gives some practical steps that can help pave the way toward empathy, compassion and ultimately forgiveness.

1. From the viewpoint of the offender, write a very descriptive letter describing the offense with details as you remember or perceived them. Explain the offender's thoughts, feelings and motives as though you were the transgressor.

2. Try to imagine what it would have been like if you were in his or her shoes. Write a descriptive e-mail from the perspective of the transgressor and then delete it.

3. Write a poem to express how the offender would have felt.

4. Make an audio tape; try to imagine the situation of the wrongdoer. Play back the tape, and confront your own resentment and bitterness.

5. Imagining yourself as the offender, write a letter of apology.

6. Talk to an understanding and discreet friend. Let her be a sounding board so you can try to understand why someone did what he did.

7. Create your own "empathy chair." Set up two chairs. Pretend you are the offender and explain to your imaginary self in the other chair why you did what you did.

8. If it is safe and appropriate to do so, actually listen to your transgressor. If you can really listen to her motives and feelings without being provoked or striking back, this could prove to be a healthy airing of differences. It could also lead to healing and forgiveness.[12]

Grace – God's Alternative

If we do not forgive, we become like the teachers and Pharisees standing around the adulterous woman. We each have a stone in our hands, ready to fling in self-righteous judgment. While our offender struggles with the speck of dust in his eye, we are blinded by the plank in our own. We can't see our faults clearly, but we are ready to expose the faults of others. We believe we are on a higher plane of goodness than "sinners."

What would have happened if those teachers and Pharisees had followed Paul's admonition to the Galatians: "Brothers, if someone is caught in a sin, you who are spiritual should restore him gently. But watch yourself, or you also may be tempted. Carry each other's burdens, and in this way you will fulfill the law of Christ" (Galatians 6:1-2). Instead of fulfilling the law of Moses by stoning someone else, we are called to help the transgressor in her weaknesses. In this way, we fulfill Christ's law.

God's grace made it possible for all people to come to Him. When we refuse to forgive others, we interfere with that grace. We are playing God in their lives by passing judgment on them. Forgiving others is a way of extending God's grace.[13] How dare we try to keep that grace only for ourselves!

Stopping to Ask

1. In the parable of the Pharisee and the tax collector in Luke 18:9-14, what basic characteristic did the praying Pharisee portray? How was his attitude like that of the teachers and Pharisees who were ready to stone the adulterous woman?

2. What effect did Christ's silent writing on the ground have on the teachers and Pharisees when they sought judgment for the adulterous woman? Why do you think that the older teachers and Pharisees slipped away before the younger ones?

3. How did Christ's treatment of the woman exemplify His teaching in Luke 6:37?

4. What is the consistent theme of these verses: Isaiah 53:6; 64:6 and Romans 3:23?

5. Who provides our defense when we sin (1 John 2:1-2)?

6. What is empathy? How can it help soften our hearts to be more forgiving?

7. What are some steps toward empathy that might help us better understand the offender?

8. How do we fulfill the law of Christ when we try to restore someone to God (Galatians 6:1-2)?

9. When Paul wrote Timothy to have nothing to do with people who are unforgiving, what other sins did he list (2 Timothy 3:1-5)?

10. How far will God's mercy be extended to us (Matthew 6:12, 14-15)?

Going Further – 2 Chronicles 28:1-15

1. Of what sins was Ahaz, king of Judah, guilty? How did Pekah, king of Israel, inflict heavy casualties on Ahaz and the people of Judah? What plunder and captives did Pekah take?

2. Who was the prophet of the Lord who met the army of Israel as it returned home with its bounty? Why did he ask, "But aren't you also guilty of sins against the Lord your God?"

3. What measures did the officials of Israel take to ensure the prisoners of Judah returned home? Why is it wise for us to consider our own failings before we condemn others?

If Jesus Died for Everyone, Why Isn't Everyone Saved?

What does Aunt Myrtle have to do with forgiveness and salvation? Plenty! Let's say that Aunt Myrtle left you $250,000 in her will. Sure, you were a nice kid, but you truly don't deserve such a generous gift even on your good days.

But there's a catch. You have to fly to Midland, Texas, to take care of the legalities in person. You can't take care of it through the mail. You must show up in the lawyer's office yourself.

I don't know about you, but I would hop on the fastest plane to Midland. Or the fastest bus. Or the fastest horse! I would somehow get to Midland and fulfill the terms that Aunt Myrtle set out. I would get fingerprints, signatures, Social Security card in order – whatever – because inheritance, here I come! I would be happy to meet the conditions in order to obtain the gift.

Think a minute about God's gift. It is an overwhelmingly generous inheritance – eternal life (Romans 6:23). It is free. We can do nothing to deserve it. We can be the nicest we can be, but we still will never deserve it. And yet, it is extended to everyone. No one is excluded from His offer. Starting with the Jews and extending to the Gentiles, everybody can take advantage of God's grace through Christ's death on the cross. Better still, God wants them to have it. He wants everyone to receive His inheritance.

You can't say that for everyone else offering his or her inheritance! God wants everyone to be saved (1 Timothy 2:3-4). "The Lord is not slow in keeping his promise, as some understand slowness. He is patient with you, not wanting anyone to perish, but everyone to come to repentance" (2 Peter 3:9). Yet in wanting everyone to be saved, God has outlined certain conditions that we need to meet to obtain His gift. He is not obligated to forgive or save the wicked. Examples abound in the Bible of those who were unwilling to follow God's conditions. Referring to the evil fallout from King Manasseh's reign, 2 Kings 24:4 states that because of Judah's evil ways "the Lord was not willing to forgive." God is willing to forgive and save only those who are willing to obey Him.[14] Those are His conditions to receive the greatest inheritance man has ever known. Isn't it worth whatever it takes?

Chapter 7

Shedding Your Baggage

*"Two of life's heaviest burdens are a chip on
the shoulder and a grudge in the heart."*
~ *Anonymous* [1]

Once an old man and his grandson were traveling with their donkey. On the way, someone said, "Look at that old man on his poor feet while that strong young man rides on the donkey!" So the man rode the donkey and the boy walked. Then the old man heard people exclaim, "Can you believe it – letting that poor boy walk all that way while that man rides free and easy!" So to please them, both the man and his grandson rode on the donkey. It wasn't long before someone said, "That poor beast is suffering under the weight of both those brutes." At that, both of them got off and walked. They walked until they heard someone mutter, "What a waste – that beast of burden should be used to carry something!" The boy ended up walking and the old man carried the donkey! [2]

Clearly that grandfather was carrying a load he didn't need to bear. We often find ourselves in the same predicament. We carry around the heavy baggage of grudges that we need to shed. We strain under the weight of feelings of resentment and ill will toward others. God asks us to lay them down, but we still struggle under our burdens, even when we could be free. Meanwhile, the burdens just grow bigger and heavier with each passing day.

We must learn to throw away our grudge baggage! With every wrong and hurt we experience, we can let our suitcase keep filling up until it overflows. Our clothes are so wrinkled we can't wear them. The suitcase is so heavy we strain our backs trying to pick it up. That's just what grudges and resentments do. They mar our appearance by wrinkling our faces, hardening our features, and drooping the corners of our mouths. Have you ever noticed what a scowl does to the face? Disfigurement by resentment can't be improved by plastic surgery because it will just come back! [3] Clearly, the way to be more beautiful – inside and out – is to shed the baggage and get on with our journey. But people can't seem to move on.

Home Is Where the Grudge Is

Grudges are apparent throughout the Bible, starting in Genesis. It didn't take long for Cain to resent his brother Abel for offering a better sacrifice. That resentment grew to hatred and finally resulted in murder. Hagar and Sarah bore ill feelings regarding their ability or inability to bear children. Then there was the running contest of baby-making between Rachel and Leah and their servants Bilhah and Zilpah. Esau had a grudge against Jacob for stealing his birthright. Jacob (along with Rachel and Leah) resented his father-in-law for treating him unfairly as an employer. Laban then resented Jacob and his family for running off without saying goodbye (and he wasn't too happy about his missing household gods either). This is not an exhaustive list, but you get the idea.

Do you notice a pattern? So many of these grudges occurred in families. Families have been fighting and harboring grudges for centuries. A friend of mine dreaded going to his family reunion because of their insidious grudges. He said by the time one side had snubbed the other side of the family, fought over the activities they had planned, and incited the children to get involved in their petty arguments, it would be worse than a pay-per-view fight. Where did this backbiting really start? Over rival football teams!

Whether the reasons are real or imagined, serious or trivial, grudges break apart families, friends, churches and even countries. Often people don't even remember why they bear a grudge. They only know they do – and nothing will change their minds. The resentment runs deep – sometimes deep enough to kill.

Not Brotherly Kindness

Imagine being hated by your big brother. Now multiply that by 10. The ultimate grudge-bearers in God's Word may have been Joseph's brothers. Favoritism was certainly a reason for their resentment. Jacob loved and favored the firstborn son of his beloved wife Rachel. His preferential treatment of Joseph galled his brothers. When they compared their robes to his exquisite one or their dreams to his grandiose visions, they always came up short.

We wonder how different all their lives would have been if Jacob had treated his children more fairly. We also wonder how Rachel and Leah's competitive spirit entered into the family one-upmanship equation. However it happened, we know that the brothers' fury was directed toward Joseph, who was the apple of his father's eye and the bane of their own. When he came looking for them in the wilderness – alone – no wonder they wanted to kill him!

They would have killed him too, had it not been for Reuben. Reuben persuaded his brothers to throw Joseph into a cistern so that he could later rescue his younger brother. Judah had the bright idea to sell him to the passing Ishmaelites. For 20 shekels of silver, the brothers were rid of their hated sibling and richer besides. On their return, they showed their father, Jacob, the blood-covered robe of Joseph. Assuming Joseph had been torn apart by some wild animal plunged the elderly patriarch into the depths of grief. The brothers said nothing to the contrary for years, watching their father suffer needlessly. We wonder if they ever questioned their motives and actions.

Years later, forced by the threat of starvation, they made a trip to Egypt. Unwittingly, they came face to face with their brother Joseph, who had a great many reasons to have a grudge against them!

Joseph's Side of the Story

In one day Joseph's life was changed forever. He was demoted from the favored son of a respected patriarch to a lowly slave. He was removed from the country of his youth to a foreign land. He was falsely accused by his master's wife and sent directly to Pharaoh's prison for at least two years where he was forgotten by the person who could have freed him. But in all this, he kept his integrity and faith in God.

He told the chief cupbearer, "For I was forcibly carried off from the land of the Hebrews, and even here I have done nothing to deserve being put in a dungeon" (Genesis 40:15).

Years later, another day changed Joseph's life again, and he was made second in command in Egypt. The tables turned, and the once slave was now sitting on a throne. It was in this position that he saw his brothers bowing before him.

Now was his chance. A lesser man might have had his brothers tortured and killed. But Joseph tested them to see if they had changed. Perhaps he was testing himself too. Was he ready to forgive their treachery? Were they ready to put away their hard feelings against him?

When he could bear it no longer, Joseph had everyone leave the room except his brothers. He began to weep and made himself known to them. A flood of emotions rushed over him. Joseph had had a lot of time to think since leaving his homeland, and during that time he made a pivotal step on the road to forgiveness. He decided to accept the pain of his experience. Instead of denying it, hiding it or transferring that pain to someone else, he decided to absorb it. Just like a sponge absorbing water until it is full, he absorbed the enormity of his pain. With the passing of time, it dissipated until he was free of it. Then he could move on to forgive and heal.[4]

The years had mellowed all of the brothers. When they finally learned the truth, they embraced with tears and then joy! Joseph explained that God's providence had been working to turn their malicious act into something worthwhile. He told them, "But God sent me ahead of you to preserve for you a remnant on earth and to save your lives by a great deliverance. So then, it was not you who sent me here, but God" (Genesis 45:7-8).

Later the brothers wondered if Joseph had been sincere. "When Joseph's brothers saw that their father was dead, they said, 'What if Joseph holds a grudge against us and pays us back for all the wrongs we did to him?' ... His brothers then came and threw themselves down before him. 'We are your slaves,' they said" (Genesis 50:15, 18). Their worries were unfounded. Joseph reassured them that he would provide for them and their children.

Shedding Excess Baggage

Not every grudge ends like this. Don't we wish they all did! What can we do to make more of them have a happy ending? How can we shed the baggage that we needlessly carry around?

• *Seek God's help in prayer.* Pray for the person or persons by name. Pray for a forgiving attitude that will help replace your negative feelings with positive ones. Resolve that with God's help you can forgive. God knows more about forgiveness than anyone else – ask His help!

• *Study God's Word* about particular examples in which people held bitterness and resentment against others. How did they succeed in overcoming these feelings? How did they fail? Concentrate on passages that detail our responsibilities to others. Memorize Bible verses that emphasize love and forgiveness.

• *Seek to make things right* with a person if he or she is aware of your hard feelings (if it is appropriate and safe to do so). If the person does not know of your grudge, settle the matter between you and God. Realize that the person might not even know you were hurt.

• *Accept the pain of your experience.* Name, own and express the hurt and don't minimize it.[5] Don't go out and seek pain, but absorb it when it comes. When you can stop denying, avoiding, repressing or ignoring the pain, you will find you can handle it, and it lessens. You don't have to transfer it to others. You don't have to keep it all inside. You can become a survivor instead of a victim. The memories and grief of loss may still be there, but you are able to move on and begin to heal.[6]

• *Physically bury your grudges.* Author Carole Mayhall tells about a friend who felt unloved by her parents. Even as an adult, she relived her broken childhood with each visit to their home. Her healing began when she wrote a list of every sin she remembered committing, including hating her mother for hating her. Over this in big letters, she wrote "FORGIVEN BY JESUS." Then she wrote a letter to her parents explaining all the hurt she felt. With the same red pen, she wrote "I FORGIVE YOU JUST AS CHRIST FORGAVE ME." Then she buried both papers in her back yard. By physically burying her "baggage," she found emotional and spiritual relief.[7]

• *Seek the counsel of a wise woman you respect.* Sometimes we are blind to the fact that our hearts might have the root of bitterness. An opinion of a nonjudgmental mentor can be invaluable. Together you can work through some of the issues you face. Sharing can show you how she might have faced similar challenges and overcome them, or perhaps you can learn from her mistakes. If you think you need more help, seek the help of a professional counselor, preferably a Christian.[8]

• *Find others to burn your grudges symbolically together.* Townspeople in the Northeastern United States come out for "Grudge-Burning Day." Leaves are raked into a huge pile. As the bonfire blazes, people throw in slips of paper with their grudges written on them. As their grudges go up in smoke, people feel much better.[9]

• *Find a symbolic shorthand as a reminder.* One lady was heartbroken that her formerly sweet-dispositioned mother now had dementia and used abusive language toward her. The granddaughter came up with an idea that helped them both. She told her to just let it fly on by and motioned with her hands a flying gesture. From then on they used that symbolic shorthand as if to say, "We're not going to let this hurt us. It's going to fly on by."[10]

• *Take positive steps to keep bitterness from taking root.* When you are tempted to grovel in the grudge pipes, do something special for someone else.[11] Go a step further and give your offender a gift.[12]

• *Remember who had a reason to really have a grudge* but chose not to. Jesus was mistreated, mocked, beaten and crucified – for no fault of His own. If anyone had a reason to harbor a grudge, He did – but He didn't (1 Peter 2:21-25)!

Charles Dickens and William Makepeace Thackery, great English literary giants of the 19th century, were estranged for several years. In London they happened to meet. Impulsively, Thackery seized Dickens' hand in friendship, and the old animosity melted. A few days afterward Thackery died, and Dickens visited his grave. An observer later wrote, "Is it not always well to seek forgiveness now?" [13] What would happen if we died today and left unsaid our words of forgiveness?

Stopping to Ask

1. How do bitterness and resentment show in our appearance?

2. Who were some people in the Bible who held grudges? What were their reasons?

3. Why did Herodias nurse a grudge against John the Baptist? What was she eventually able to do to him (Mark 6:14-29)?

4. What part did Jacob's treatment of Joseph play in Joseph's brothers' grudge? What other reasons did Joseph's brothers have for resenting Joseph?

5. What reason did Joseph have for resenting his brothers? What helped Joseph see the reason he was brought to Egypt?

6. Why did the brothers doubt Joseph's forgiveness when Jacob died?

7. How can prayer and Bible study about forgiveness help us carry through with our own forgiveness?

8. If appropriate and safe, why is it important to settle a grudge with a person as soon as you can?

9. In working through forgiveness, why is it better to absorb pain rather than to ignore, repress, avoid or deny it?

10. What are some other ways mentioned in the chapter to help us shed our grudges?

Going Further – Numbers 12

1. Why did Miriam and Aaron speak against Moses? What did God do to demonstrate His power and His confidence in Moses?

2. Why do you think God was so angry with Miriam and Aaron? What happened to Miriam?

3. What did Aaron beg of Moses? How did Moses respond? What qualities did he exemplify?

4. What did God require of Miriam? Why do we assume she was healed?

5. When friends and family needlessly criticize us, what can help us be more forgiving?

How Can We Forget a Minor Offense Against Us?

An interesting thing about humans is that often when we want to remember something, it flits away, leaving our memory blank. But when we want to forget something, it often stays locked in our brain like a stubborn stain on our favorite shirt.

It's often that way when you want to forget a minor offense someone has committed against you. Maybe you have tried to dismiss it, but still the hurt keeps popping up in your memory. The harder you try to forget, the more entrenched the slight becomes. With each replay of the event, the more serious it grows.

Several memory triggers might make forgetting a minor offense difficult. If circumstances make it necessary to see the offending person often, you might be reminded constantly of the hurt. But the opposite can also be true. You might not see that person often, but when you do, the memories linked to the pain suddenly return. Or you might see another person who treated you the same way the first person did and the feelings of unforgiveness come back.[14]

We can choose to ruminate on a minor breach, or we can take it as part of our sinful humanity and move on. Perhaps we were having a bad day, or maybe we caught the other person at a bad time. Whether the slight was intended or not, we can actively choose not to rehearse it on the center stage of our minds. Instead of worrying about forgetting an offense, we can remember our decision to forgive.[15] Perhaps we will always remember but not with the same negative feelings. When Clara Barton was reminded of an offense against her, she reportedly said, "I distinctly remember forgetting it."[16]

We should strive to love people with a love that is not easily provoked (1 Corinthians 13:5). We need to try harder to get over the small offenses in our everyday lives. Sometimes these little things can be irritating, just like grains of sand in our shoes, but we need to be mature enough to move on and overlook them (Proverbs 19:11). If we don't, we will just be making mountains out of molehills, and we don't need any more mountains in the journey of life![17]

Chapter 8

Maneuvering Around the Potholes

*"Forgiveness is not a way; it is the way. It is the only way
for the Lord or for us to deal with a sinful, guilty past."*
~ Helen W. Kooiman [1]

R oy Merritt in his book *Potholes: Ups and Downs on Zambia's
Mission Road* tells about the dangers of driving on unlighted Zambian
roads at night. First he must avoid the lorries (trucks) speeding at 80 miles
per hour. Then he barely misses other lorries parked in the road with
no headlights! Meanwhile he has to weave back and forth between me-
andering drunks, wandering animals and darting charcoal bikes. But there
is one thing he is certain to encounter on every road he travels – potholes.
He has to maneuver around the salad-bowl-sized potholes, kitchen-sink-
sized potholes, washing-machine-sized potholes, Jacuzzi-sized potholes,
swimming-pool-sized potholes, and "a few Really BIG Potholes." [2]

Guilt is a lot like those potholes. It can work its way to the surface
on every road we travel, and the road to forgiveness is no exception.
Like potholes, we often don't take the time and effort to fix guilt. Instead
of doing something about it, we ignore it or try to cover it up. It erodes
deeper and wider until we feel like we are going to fall in and get lost.

We can do something about guilt, but we need help. Just as potholes
filled with loose gravel soon wear out again, so it is with our guilt. We
need more than a temporary quick fix. We need some serious repair
work, and we need it now!

Guilt Away

Jesus Christ is the only one who can really fix our guilt. He had no reason to be guilty because He lived a sinless life. He encountered every kind of temptation we do, yet was able to resist them all (Hebrews 4:15). He did not need forgiveness because He had no sins to forgive.

We are a different story. We are tempted, and often we fail. Our feelings of guilt are justified because we are guilty.[3] We have all done things we are ashamed to admit. A London playwright supposedly sent messages anonymously to 20 prominent citizens: "All has been found out. Leave town at once." All 20 left the city that night![4]

Our sins separate us from God. Isaiah makes it plain:

> Surely the arm of the Lord is not too short to save, nor his ear too dull to hear. But your iniquities have separated you from your God; your sins have hidden his face from you, so that he will not hear. For your hands are stained with blood, your fingers with guilt. Your lips have spoken lies, and your tongue mutters wicked things. ... Our offenses are ever with us, and we acknowledge our iniquities. (Isaiah 59:1-3, 12b)

Sin brought us guilt and separation from God, but Christ brought cleansing and reconciliation. Jesus bridged the enormous gap between man and God. Through God's Son, our consciences can be cleansed so we don't have to feel guilty anymore. We can be forgiven. "How much more, then, will the blood of Christ, who through the eternal Spirit offered himself unblemished to God, cleanse our consciences from acts that lead to death, so that we may serve the living God ... [L]et us draw near to God with a sincere heart in full assurance of faith, having our hearts sprinkled to cleanse us from a guilty conscience and having our bodies washed with pure water" (Hebrews 9:14; 10:22).

Sometimes it's difficult to convince ourselves that we can be forgiven and our guilt can be taken away. We get entrenched in it and can't seem to escape. Just like those African potholes, we won't always escape guilt because we will be guilty sometimes. But we don't have to stay guilty. There is no way to get around some potholes because sin and its consequences are real. Unfortunately, some potholes we actually dig for ourselves!

Guilt Trips and Other Detours

Sometimes as Christians we feel guilty when we are not guilty in God's sight. Either from a misunderstanding of God's grace or an oversensitive conscience, we feel God's wrath for what we have or have not done. Sometimes we need to go along the road of guilt, but a "guilt trip" is an unnecessary detour into false guilt.

Survivors of violence and abuse often suffer from guilt trips. For example, victims of incest may believe that their experience was their fault. They may even convince themselves that they were willing participants. A little girl may want her father's attention. He tells her what they do is her fault, and she believes him. She is too afraid to resist or tell. Although she thinks it is wrong, she really is not able to protect herself. She suffers from false guilt. She is not guilty of wrongdoing, yet often lives a lifetime of guilt and shame.[5]

Robert Enright in his book *Forgiveness Is a Choice* defines the difference between shame and guilt: "Shame is the fear of what others will think when they find out what has happened to us. Guilt is how we feel about ourselves when we realize that we have violated our own standards of right and wrong."[6] We read about people in the Bible who suffered from both of these feelings, but some had no reason to feel guilty. In fact, some were trying to do the right thing, but their worlds were turned upside down by the foolishness of others. For example, Tamar, King David's daughter and Ammon's half-sister, was only following her father's request to prepare a meal for her "sick" half-brother when Ammon savagely raped her.

When things go wrong in our lives, we might think God is punishing us. But Paul tells us that if we are in the right relationship in Christ, we don't have to feel guilty: "Therefore, there is now no condemnation for those who are in Christ Jesus" (Romans 8:1). We can also find peace: "Therefore, since we have been justified through faith, we have peace with God through our Lord Jesus Christ" (5:1). If we are suffering from a guilt trip, we need to reexamine our lives, repent of and confess any sins, and then know that God has taken them away.[7]

If we are truly guilty, we don't want to stay that way. Unresolved guilt can gnaw away at our insides, until we too are destroyed. Joseph's brothers showed how their guilt had never gone away but probably tormented them over the years. When they stood before Joseph, the ruler of Egypt, they found themselves admitting their guilt to each other, unaware that their brother understood every word. "They said to one another, 'Surely we are being punished because of our brother. We saw how distressed he was when he pleaded with us for his life, but we would not listen; that's why this distress has come upon us.' Reuben replied, 'Didn't I tell you not to sin against the boy? But you wouldn't listen! Now we must give an accounting for his blood' " (Genesis 42:21-22). They had been silently steeping in their own self-blame for years. Fortunately, they were able to resolve it. But think of all the years they wasted! Two other men dealt with their guilt in a different way.

Sinking Pretty Low

They were alike and yet so different. They were handpicked by their master. They were chosen for roles of responsibility in their group. They ate and worked together for about three years. They were both outspoken. They both carried enormous loads of guilt. And both were justified in feeling that way because their actions were despicable. But their reaction to that guilt led them down entirely different paths.

Peter, a disciple in Christ's inner circle, witnessed amazing miracles not seen by the other disciples. He was the most outspoken of the group; it was no surprise that he claimed that he would be ready to go with his Lord to prison and death. In the shadows of the Garden of Gethsemane in an impetuous act of bravery, Peter cut off the ear of Malchus, the servant of the high priest. But when Jesus was arrested, Peter fled the scene with the other disciples.

At Jesus' trial, when Peter was accused three times of being with Jesus, he denied his association each time. After the third time, the rooster crowed, and Jesus turned and looked pointedly at Peter. What a look of disappointment that must have been! Peter went out and wept bitterly. His tears demonstrated that he felt his guilt deeply.

How did he handle that guilt? He remained with the disciples despite his mistake and witnessed the resurrected Lord. He later received a threefold personal affirmation that Christ had forgiven him and had plans for him in the kingdom. Peter went on to preach the first gospel sermon on Pentecost and serve as a leader in the church after it was established. Peter sought and received forgiveness and moved beyond his guilt to be reconciled with God.

In contrast, Judas dealt with his guilt much differently. Jesus saw Judas' potential, but He also knew what he was. This disciple served as treasurer of the 12 apostles, but he embezzled money from the group. Judas was vocal in criticizing Mary for anointing Jesus' feet with costly ointment. He claimed that the money spent should go to the poor, but in reality he wanted to dip into the funds himself. He took advantage of the opportunity to make 30 pieces of silver – the price of a slave – but this money was for the betrayal of the Lord.[8]

As a last gesture of friendship at the Last Supper, Jesus honored Judas by handing him the piece of bread which He had dipped in the dish.[9] Ironically, the Lord was also signifying who should betray Him. Then Judas set out to accomplish his treacherous task.

Jesus called Judas "a devil" (John 6:70), and the disciple certainly acted like one when he led the officials and soldiers to arrest the Lord. Feigning affection, he betrayed Christ with a kiss. When he realized that the Romans would surely crucify Jesus, he returned the money to the Jewish leaders, but it was too late. " 'I have sinned,' he said, 'for I have betrayed innocent blood.' 'What is that to us?' they replied. 'That's your responsibility' " (Matthew 27:4). Throwing the money into the temple, he went out and hanged himself.

Both men were remorseful for what they had done. One went on to be forgiven by Jesus. The other felt that forgiveness was unattainable. He felt his guilt was too great. God could have forgiven him, but he could not forgive himself.

The Hardest Person to Forgive

So many people today cannot forgive themselves. They can't seem to shake off the weight of guilt, even after they have repented and asked forgiveness. They think their sin is too heinous, their blunder too hurtful or far-reaching. They suffer from an unresolved guilt that totally engulfs their lives. If they allow that guilt to keep hanging over them, it can break them physically, emotionally and spiritually. Estimates indicate that 70 percent of mental ward patients today could be released if they could only find forgiveness.[10]

People throughout the ages have tried to resolve their guilt by any means possible. When the Black Plague was raging in Europe in the 13th century, a fanatical sect called the Flagellants held long processions throughout the cities and towns. This heretical cult filed down the streets naked, beating themselves with rods, whips and chains and lacerating their bleeding bodies. Why did they display such self-mutilation? They thought that only by suffering so cruelly could they be forgiven of their sins.[11]

We find it incredible that people in the past could be so self-destructive. But how often do we succumb to self-punishing behaviors to find some way to atone for our sins and find peace?

A 76-year-old lady made an appointment to speak with her preacher. As tears filled her eyes, this sweet little lady admitted having a one-time sexual encounter with a coworker. She had asked her husband's forgiveness and he granted it, but she could not forgive herself. After years of dedicated service to God, she still believed she would go to hell for her sin of adultery. How could she ever be good enough to make up for that sin? She could not understand how God could grant her forgiveness, even after many years of asking Him for that precious gift.

The preacher read her Paul's description of first-century pagans: sexually immoral, idolaters, adulterers, male prostitutes, homosexual offenders, thieves, greedy, drunkards, slanderers and swindlers (1 Corinthians 6:9-10). Those listed would certainly not go to heaven. Then he read Paul's description of the change in the Corinthians' lives: "And that is what some of you were. But you were washed, you were sanctified, you were justified in the name of the Lord Jesus Christ and by the Spirit of our God" (v. 11). The preacher then asked her, "Now do you think that God's grace cannot wash, sanctify and justify you?" She was finally convinced that God's abounding love and forgiveness extended to her and happily she could be free of guilt.

We say, and rightly so, that we don't deserve forgiveness. That's the point. If we did deserve it, we would not need it! We can never be good enough. Guilt cannot atone for our sins. Only one Person can.[12]

Christ has already paid the price for our sins, and yet we often continue to try to pay for them ourselves. Are we telling Jesus that His grace is not sufficient for us? If He has forgiven us, then we can accept

His grace and forgive ourselves. As author Ron Lee Davis aptly put it, "If you believe your sins are too great for God to forgive, then your God is too small! The true living God of the Bible offers grace upon grace upon grace, and His grace is greater than all our sins!" [13]

Stopping to Ask

1. How does the Bible take the idea of cleansing a guilty conscience in Hebrews 10:22 a step further in 1 Peter 3:21?

2. Even after Joseph forgave them, how did his brothers show that they still felt guilty for what they had done to him (Genesis 42:21)?

3. What separates and alienates man from God (Isaiah 59:1-3; Colossians 1:21)?

4. Who is the solution to our sin problem (Romans 3:21-26)?

5. What is the difference between shame and guilt?

6. What is false guilt? What is an example of someone who suffers from false guilt?

7. If we are trying to live godly lives, why is there no need to feel guilty (Romans 5:1-2; 8:1-2)?

8. How did Peter and Judas react differently to their guilt?

9. Why is it sometimes hardest to forgive ourselves?

10. Do you think the people mentioned in the six references given here felt guilt, shame or both? How did they express these feelings?

Tamar (2 Samuel 13:1-22):	Shame	Guilt
Expression _____		
Ninevites (Jonah 3:3-10):	Shame	Guilt
Expression _____		
Pilate (Matthew 27:11-26):	Shame	Guilt
Expression _____		

Jews at Pentecost (Acts 2:36-41):	Shame	Guilt

Expression _____

Simon the Sorcerer (Acts 8:9-24):	Shame	Guilt

Expression _____

Ephesian sorcerers (Acts 19:11-20):	Shame	Guilt

Expression _____

Going Further – Guilt Offerings

1. When the children of Israel offered a guilt offering, what was the procedure they had to follow (Leviticus 7:1-10)? What offerings were required for these sins?

    a. desecrating holy things (5:14-16)

    b. unintentionally sinning (5:17-19)

    c. deceiving or cheating a neighbor (6:1-7)

    d. seducing a slave girl (19:20-22)

2. Who became our guilt offering (Isaiah 53:10)? Why should this make us more fully appreciate Christ's once-for-all sacrifice (Hebrews 9:11-10:18)?

Do Flashbacks Mean
I Am Not Forgiven?

"How can I know I am forgiven when I still have flashbacks from my past? Does that mean my forgiveness from God is invalid?" A Christian lady asked her preacher these questions when she continued to have memories from an earlier illicit affair. She had asked forgiveness from God, her husband, and the church, but she still got random images of her sinful actions at inopportune times – in worship, in her Bible study, even in intimate moments with her husband! How could she be forgiven?

Her preacher explained that memories of our sinful pasts are powerful, and they can make us doubt our forgiveness from God. But it should give us comfort to realize that memories, or the lack of them, do not determine our forgiveness. There is an important difference between forgetting and forgiving.[14]

Our brains are marvelous memory storage tanks, storing at least 600 memories a second. That translates to 1.5 trillion bits of information gathered by the time we reach the age of 75. All these bits are relayed by chemical transfer and electronic impulses. Memory is a biological function, not a spiritual one. [15] We cannot consciously purge our memories, even if we tried. (If you don't believe that, try consciously to forget something!)

Although we may not be able to remember some events in our lives, they are recorded in our brain and might resurface at any time. That is probably why Paul must have chafed at the memories of his past deeds. Although he could not totally erase them from his memory, he chose not to let them drag him down – "Forgetting what is behind and straining toward what is ahead" (Philippians 3:13). He even sometimes found it beneficial to remember what he formerly was – a blasphemer, a persecutor and a violent man. Yet he also could thank God for His mercy and demonstrate to others that if God could forgive him, He could forgive them (1 Timothy 1:12-16).

In the same way, we can learn to benefit from our past memories. When they appear uninvited, we can know they do not invalidate our forgiveness. More than ever, we can thank God and confidently say with Paul, "The grace of our Lord was poured out on me abundantly, along with the faith and love that are in Christ Jesus" (1 Timothy 1:14).[16]

Chapter 9

Lost and Going in Circles

"How many times do you have to sin before God doesn't love you?"
~ Unknown

F ew things are more frustrating than being lost. In unfamiliar ter-
rain, we can get disoriented easily. Sometimes it is only by plung-
ing ahead with dead reckoning or relying on that dreaded last resort –
asking for directions – that we find our way.

Often we keep making the same mistakes in navigation. If we don't
know where we are going, what keeps us from treading the same wrong
path again – especially in the dark? It's no surprise when we end up
where we started! We're lost and going in circles.

The same is true for people who are spiritually lost. Since they have
lost a sense of spiritual direction, what keeps them from making the
same mistakes? They tread the sinful path again and again – and still
need forgiveness over and over.

Setting a Limit

Perhaps this was what Peter was thinking about when he asked Jesus
about forgiveness. "Lord, how many times shall I forgive my brother
when he sins against me? Up to seven times?" (Matthew 18:21). Peter
was asking if there was a limit to our responsibility to forgive others.
The Jewish rabbis taught that men should forgive three offenses but
stop at the fourth one. Peter might have thought himself generous for
increasing the rabbis' three to seven.[1]

But instead of commending Peter, Jesus answered him "seventy-seven times" or "seventy times seven." The numeric expression here was a typical Jewish way to say, "Never hold grudges."[2] Scholars disagree on the literal translation of the number, but the exact number is not important. Who's counting after 77 anyway! We are not limited by 77 or 490, by quantity or frequency. The point is that no matter how often we are offended, Jesus calls us to forgive.[3]

Our Lord illustrated His point by launching into the parable of the unmerciful servant, contrasting the exorbitant debt of the first servant with the measly debt of the second servant. He demonstrated the great debt we owe God for forgiving our sins, giving us reason to forgive others their offenses. God has forgiven us much more than we can ever forgive someone else!

Seven Times a Day

In a related passage, Jesus approached forgiveness from a different direction. He told His disciples, "So watch yourselves. If your brother sins, rebuke him, and if he repents, forgive him. If he sins against you seven times in a day, and seven times comes back to you and says, 'I repent,' forgive him" (Luke 17:3-4). The Lord reminds us that rebuking is as important as forgiving but neither is a one-time experience. We are to do it as often as necessary. Again, Christ is not picking a specific number but rather saying that there should be no limit to our forgiveness.

How do we put this over-and-over-again-forgiveness into practice? Isn't that asking too much of us? Apparently the disciples thought so too, for they asked Jesus, "Increase our faith!" They thought they needed more faith for such a difficult task. They might have wondered how they could continue to forgive.

It might be really difficult to forgive some people just once but to keep on forgiving them – almost impossible! But look at how Jesus was mistreated in one day – betrayed, forsaken, denied, misjudged, rejected, mocked, beaten and crucified. Yet He still exhibited a forgiving attitude: "Father, forgive them, for they do not know what they are doing" (Luke 23:34).

It is easy to judge a person in a certain situation and tell her she needs to keep forgiving. But how easy is it for you to forgive over and over if:

- your preschool niece spills milk on your carpet again?
- your cutthroat coworker continues to make your job difficult?
- your mother embarrasses you again in front of your friends?
- your father comes home from another drinking binge?
- your husband has been caught with yet another women?

One husband found himself in a similar predicament. His wife bore at least two of three children who were not his own. She finally left him for the arms of another man. Despite this, her husband still loved her. He brought her back home and forgave her. He knew what she had become, but he loved her anyway!

Hosea's Love

Popular books have chronicled the painful experience of a faithful spouse lamenting a wayward mate, but none of these is quite like the book of Hosea. In it, God commands the prophet Hosea to marry "an adulterous wife" (Hosea 1:2). Why would God ask Hosea to marry a woman like this? God weaves His will to illustrate His point graphically: He still loved the idolatrous nation of Israel. His unfailing love for adulterous Israel is mirrored in the abiding love that Hosea had for his wife, Gomer.

Some commentators think that Gomer was already a prostitute when Hosea married her. Perhaps she was a temple prostitute in the erotic cultic worship of that time. From its initial introduction by Jeroboam I to the northern kingdom of Israel, idol worship was widespread and morals had decayed. By Hosea's time, Canaanite influences had integrated idolatry and sexual debauchery into the worship of God. Orgies and drunkenness were characteristic of the high places and local shrines dedicated to the pagan gods and goddesses. The fertility of the land, people, and even animals were linked to the sexual activity of the fertility god Baal and goddess Asherah. Erotic acts performed by male and female prostitutes supposedly stimulated these gods, which in turn made the land fertile to produce a bountiful harvest. It is possible that Gomer participated in these sinful practices (Hosea 4:10-19).[4]

Other commentators think that Gomer was chaste when she married Hosea and later was influenced by a nation "guilty of the vilest adultery in departing from the Lord" (Hosea 1:2). Idolatry and evil were so widespread that it would be very difficult to escape their effects. Gomer's purity when she was first married to Hosea would have presented a striking parallel to God's relationship to His chosen people when they were first brought out of Egypt (11:1; Exodus 4:22; Jeremiah 2:2-3). In the wilderness they wandered in circles of sin as well as in circles in the desert. Later they repeatedly prostituted themselves to other gods in the time of the judges and prophets. The Israelites would be oppressed because of their sins, then beg for God's mercy and forgiveness. Over and over, they strayed, returned to God, and then strayed again. Time and time again, God extended His love and mercy to Israel but she continued to wander unfaithfully from Him in spiritual adultery.[5]

Children Unloved and Loved

The naming of Gomer's three children paralleled the rift in Hosea's relationship with her and mirrored God's relationship with Israel. The names were symbolic, and each name pointed to a specific aspect in Israel's history. The first son was called Jezreel, meaning "God will scatter" or "God will sow."[6] God would "scatter" His people in captivity but eventually bring or "sow" them back to Himself. This also was related to the city of Jezreel. There Jehu obeyed God by slaughtering the house of Ahab but killed more than God commanded (2 Kings 9:1ff; Hosea 1:4). The punishment for Jehu's sin would be the "scattering" of Israel as a nation in 722 B.C.[7]

The next two children were probably not Hosea's. The second child was a daughter called Lo-Ruhamah, meaning "not loved." This shows that God's long-suffering love would no longer be shown to Israel but would manifest itself in judgment for the disobedient nation. The last child, a son born after Lo-Ruhamah was weaned, was Lo-Ammi, meaning "not my people" (Hosea 1:6-8). Israel had long departed from their Father God. They were not His people, and He was not their God. Notice the progression in separation from God through these names: being scattered, being unloved, then being disowned.[8]

Yet in all this, God looked to the day when Israel and Judah would again be united as His people and all peoples could be called God's children (Hosea 1:10-2:1). God's love would make it possible for Jews and Gentiles to be God's people. Paul reiterated this in Romans 9:25-26:

As he [God] says in Hosea: "I will call them 'my people' who are not my people; and I will call her 'my loved one' who is not my loved one," and, "It will happen that in the very place where it was said to them, 'You are not my people,' they will be called 'sons of the living God.'"

Just as God longed to be reconciled with Israel, so Hosea longed to be with his wife, Gomer, again. So God told Hosea to find his wife and bring her home. He told Hosea, "Love her as the Lord loves the Israelites, though they turn to other gods and love the sacred raisin cakes" (Hosea 3:1). At whatever point Gomer became adulterous, Hosea showed his loved for her – even to the point of buying her back for 15 shekels of silver and about a homer and a lethek of barley, an approximate amount due for redeeming a slave (Hosea 1:2; Exodus 21:32). Perhaps she had a debt she could not pay and had to become a bond-servant.[9] Hosea had the legal right to divorce her, but he chose instead to bring her home.[10]

Remembering the Hurt

No doubt Hosea spent lonely days and nights when scenes of hurt and betrayal played over and over in his mind. At times he might have questioned whether his wife would even want to return home. But he had a deep, overwhelming love for his wayward wife, and he was willing to forgive.

While Hosea's love and forgiveness for Gomer are unusual and exceptional, he was called by God to his life and his wife. Today each human relationship should be prayerfully brought before the Lord. God does not call us to remain in or return to relationships in the name of love and forgiveness when abuse or danger is involved. If you are in such a situation, find someone you trust to talk with and pray about it. While love can forgive wrongs, it does not sanction abuse or ignore danger.

But someone might say that love is not supposed to keep a record of wrongs (1 Corinthians 13:5). That is true to a certain extent. We are not to keep a tally of sins on others in our personal notebooks. At the same time, we are given memories for a purpose, and that is to protect ourselves against harm. Our brains are wired to remember serious offenses. The sound of someone's voice, the sight of his or her face, the act of harm, the resulting fearful or angry emotions – these are recorded permanently. Sometimes we only feel the pain and don't know why. At other times the painful emotions combine with the memories. [11]

Forgiveness does not automatically stop these memories of serious hurt and their attached emotions, and we do not want to stop them. Those memories prevent us from trusting someone who does not deserve to be trusted. What forgiveness can do is replace the unforgiving emotions of anger, hatred, resentment and bitterness with positive ones of empathy, compassion and love. [12]

How can we let go of the nagging memories that may continue to pop up in our minds? One way to break the chain of brooding is to consciously limit it. Limit thinking about the incident to two minutes and time yourself. Conclude with a prayer that God will help you release the hurt through a forgiving attitude as He displays with us. Then move on with all your heart. [13]

Could Hosea have forgiven Gomer and taken her back home if he had continued to brood on and cling to painful memories? He may have kept on involuntarily having waves of hurt, but he didn't have to hold on and embrace them. He refused to be immobilized by the pain of his past. He personified Peter's statement about love: "Above all, love each other deeply, because love covers over a multitude of sins" (1 Peter 4:8).

Returning Home

Returning home – the rest of the book of Hosea paints that picture for the wayward nation of Israel. After cataloging their sins and listing their punishment, God bids them to return to Him, but they refuse to come. Yet His offer of love remains even in the last chapter of the book:

> Return, O Israel, to the Lord your God. Your sins have been your downfall! Take words with you and return to the Lord. Say to him: "Forgive all our sins and receive us graciously, that we may offer the fruit of our lips." ... "I will heal their waywardness and love them freely, for my anger has turned away from them" (Hosea 14:1-2, 4).

Abundant love and forgiveness – that's what God wants for us. Hosea serves as a graphic picture of God's love and grace that stretched even back to the Old Testament. No matter how often we sin, He still offers us a chance to return and change. God's loving-kindness is always there to forgive us if we are ready to repent.

Stopping to Ask

1. What does the numeric expression in Matthew 18:22 mean to the typical Jew?

2. What marital relationship mirrored God's love for Israel?

3. In what immoral practices were the pagan temple prostitutes involved?

4. What supposedly stimulated the pagan gods to make the land fertile?

5. What were the names of Gomer's children? What did they mean? How were their meanings parallel to God's relationship to Israel?

6. In Romans 9:25-26, what did God long for Israel and Judah to be?

7. What did God tell Hosea to do with Gomer after she left him? How much did he pay?

8. What is the message of the rest of the book of Hosea?

9. "While love can forgive wrongs, it does not sanction abuse or ignore danger." Does this statement contradict 1 Peter 4:8?

10. Why do you think our brains permanently record serious painful experiences?

Going Further – Judges 2:8-23

1. What was the "sin cycle" that the Israelites went through repeatedly after Joshua's death? Why did they forsake God?

2. Why did God raise up judges to rescue them from their oppressors even when they forgot Him? What did God decide about the idolatrous nations left in Canaan? Do you think God was willing to forgive the Israelites if they repented?

3. Can you think of times when God remembered you even though you forgot Him? Was He willing to forgive you when you repented?

Does God Give Up on the Wicked?

"To do what ought not to be done" – if evil people had a mission statement, that phrase in Romans 1:28 might be it! The activities of the wicked involve all shades and types of sins. Sometimes ancient Jewish, Greek and Roman writers made lists of these sins called "vice lists." [14] Paul made his own list in Romans 1:29-31, enumerating wickedness in its varied forms: "They have become filled with every kind of wickedness, evil, greed and depravity. They are full of envy, murder, strife, deceit and malice. They are gossips, slanderers, God-haters, insolent, arrogant and boastful; they invent ways of doing evil; they disobey their parents; they are senseless, faithless, heartless, ruthless."

What prompted Paul to provide such an extensive list? He probably saw the moral decadence of these sins every day as he traveled all over the pagan world. The Greek and Roman cultures were steeped in idolatry and every kind of selfish desire. Paul was eager to travel to Rome to preach the gospel there because he knew the gospel was the only way to save the wicked people he described from their sins. [15]

Earlier in Romans, Paul explained how God had demonstrated His power through nature, but evil men had refused to acknowledge Him. They chose rather to worship idols – "created things rather than the Creator" (Romans 1:25). As their selfish desires went rampant, one sin led to another, eventually spiraling to destruction. In this context Paul says, "God gave them over" three times in downward progression (vv. 24, 26, 28). The meaning of the Greek word here conveys the idea of delivering up or over to the practice or power of something or someone. [16] Men were so vile that God allowed them to go headlong into the destruction of their sins.

It's similar to the idea in Psalm 81:11-12: "But my people would not listen to me; Israel would not submit to me. So I gave them over to their stubborn hearts to follow their own devices." Later in that passage God says how He would care for His people if they would only turn to Him. God is patient. An escape from the downward spiral of sin is available to anyone willing to break out of its tailspin.

Part Three:

On the Road Again

Horatio Nelson Jackson gave new meaning to the expression "back on the road again." In fact, this pioneer in automotive history made some of his own roads! In America in 1903, few paved roads existed – only about 150 miles – and those were within the bounds of city limits. In his adventurous trek from San Francisco to New York City, Jackson got mired in buffalo wallows and sand drifts and had to be towed out with the lariats of cowboys. To cross major rivers, he jostled over railroad trestles. Because no stores were selling car parts along the way, he endured days of delays from breakdowns and flat tires. Fascinated onlookers directed him out of his way so their relatives could see his strange contraption that sped through town at 20 miles per hour. Yet despite all these setbacks, he became the first person to cross the United States in a newfangled horseless carriage or, as one headline proclaimed, "A Real Live Auto." It only took 63 and a half days![1]

It took real spunk to finish what he had started. It is the same on our trip – to finish the journey and reach our goal of forgiveness, we need to focus on our destination. Sometimes we get discouraged, but we need to get back on the road again.

Chapter 10

Making a U-Turn

"The lowest gutter is not too low for Him."
~ Joy Haney [1]

What would we do without freeways? Where else can we cruise along at high speeds with extra lanes for slower traffic and no traffic lights to hinder us? When we have to get somewhere fast, their limited access entrance and exit ramps are a real boon.

All this works well until we need to go in the opposite direction. If we have an emergency and realize we are going the wrong way, we might panic. Whatever the problem, we need to turn around fast and go back with no time to lose.

How are we going to get to the other side? We can't drive over barriers or through fences. Driving several miles to find the next exit will take valuable minutes we can't spare. Maybe, just maybe, there is an alternative. We frantically search for a u-turn, a road to bridge one direction of highway to the other. We are grateful when we find that break in the median we need.

It's good to be able to turn around and go the opposite way spiritually too. When we finally realize we are going the wrong way, we need something to link us back to where we belong. That process of turning around and going the other way is repentance.

The original Hebrew and Greek words for repentance are translated "turn," "return," "turn away," "turn again," and "turn back." We see these in the Old and New Testaments, reverberating through the preaching of the prophets, John the Baptist, Jesus and the apostles. In essence they all preached, "Turn from sin and return to God." [2] King Solomon delineated the turning process when he prayed to God about the future of his people in captivity: "and if they have a change of heart in the land where they are held captive, and repent and plead with you in the land of their conquerors and say, 'We have sinned, we have done wrong, we have acted wickedly'; and if they turn back to you with all their heart and soul" (1 Kings 8:47-48). Repentance is the total turnaround.

The Total Turnaround

Nowhere is this turnaround seen more prominently in the Bible than in the life of Paul. His background gave him a potential one-way ticket to religious prominence and prestige. Born a Roman citizen in the busy seaport of Tarsus, he was later educated at the feet of the well-known Jewish rabbi Gamaliel in Jerusalem. He described himself as "a Hebrew of Hebrews; in regard to the law, a Pharisee; as for zeal, persecuting the church; as for legalistic righteousness, faultless" (Philippians 3:5-6).

In the first mention of Paul (Saul) in the Bible, we see him consenting to the stoning of Stephen, the first martyr of the church (Acts 8:1). With feverish zeal, Paul planned to travel to Damascus to capture Christians and drag them back to Jerusalem as prisoners. On his way there, he was blinded by a bright light and heard the voice of Jesus. This encounter with the Lord changed his life forever. After spending three days in prayer and the soul-searching realization that he was headed in the wrong direction with his life, he repented and was baptized by Ananias. He found forgiveness for his sins and began a life diametrically opposed to his former self. He immediately started preaching that Jesus is the Son of God (Acts 9:1-31).

The Jews at Damascus were baffled by Paul's transformation. Instead of being their comrade in arms, he had become one of those dreaded Christians himself! After a time, the Jews conspired to kill him, but he escaped by being lowered in a basket over the wall of the city. Now the persecutor had become the persecuted. Here was a definite turnaround!

In the years to come, waves of guilt must have resurfaced in Paul's heart. No doubt he remembered standing by in agreement as Stephen was being stoned and then rising up in persecution against other

Christians. Perhaps family members and friends of Stephen stood by him now as brothers and sisters as he preached the good news. Some of those people might have found it difficult to forgive him.

Paul probably found it difficult to forgive himself. He looked back on those years of misdirected zeal with sorrow as he described himself: "wretched man" (Romans 7:24), "worst of sinners" (1 Timothy 1:16), and "less than the least of all God's people" (Ephesians 3:8). Yet, though he saw himself at the bottom of the barrel, he knew that God had forgiven even him with all his sin. He spoke about the grace of God as one who knew what it meant to be forgiven: "For I am the least of the apostles and do not even deserve to be called an apostle, because I persecuted the church of God. But by the grace of God I am what I am, and his grace to me was not without effect. No, I worked harder than all of them – yet not I, but the grace of God that was with me" (1 Corinthians 15:9-10).

Only God's forgiveness and grace could cover Paul's past as a murderer and persecutor of the Lord's people. After escaping from Damascus he tried to join the disciples of Jerusalem, but they were afraid of him and didn't believe he was really a disciple or that his faith was sincere. It took Barnabas to convince them that he truly had repented.

A Modern U-Turn

Just as they were then, we are often skeptical today when a person leaves a life of sin and makes a complete turnaround to serve the Lord. An example of this is Jeffrey Dahmer, the convicted serial killer and cannibal. Many, including those in the church, thought his conversion to Christ was insincere. The minister who baptized Jeffrey disagreed.

Roy Ratcliff, the minister of the church of Christ in Madison, Wis., was notified that Jeffrey desired to be baptized in prison. Jeffrey had studied Bible correspondence courses from Curtis Booth and Mary Mott. These two Christians thought he was worth saving, and they were thrilled at his response. Roy made arrangements to baptize Jeffrey in the prison whirlpool tub.

Many people questioned Jeffrey's sincerity. One profanity-laced message on the church answering machine said Roy was foolish to baptize such a man. But the minister was convinced by Jeffrey's words and actions that he was sincere. Roy asked, "Can an evil person turn to God? ... What part of the blood of Christ can't save him, but can save you?"[3] His 16 life sentences would never be shortened, and he accepted the fact that he would die in prison. Jeffrey had nothing to gain in this life by repenting. But he had everything to gain in the next life.[4]

The next life for Jeffrey came sooner than anyone thought. On Nov. 28, 1994, he was beaten and killed by an inmate while they cleaned a prison gymnasium bathroom. His death came as a surprise to Roy and Jeffrey's family. Roy wrote, "Jeff was beginning to embrace the Christian spirit. His father and several pen pals saw a major transformation in who he was after he became a Christian."[5]

Just like the apostle Paul, Jeffrey Dahmer showed us that God accepts all of us, regardless of who we are or what we have done, if we are willing to repent and obey His Word. None of us are so lost in darkness that God's Word cannot pierce through it to show us the way to the light. No matter how deep we are in sin, even if we think we are unreachable, God sent His Son to save us. He can reach us. "Surely the arm of the Lord is not too short to save, nor his ear too dull to hear" (Isaiah 59:1). We just need to turn around and turn over our life to Him.

Genuine Repentance

It is important to pay attention to how we turn around. It's like the little girl who listened to her Bible teacher tell how Lot's wife looked back and turned into a pillar of salt. The little girl exclaimed, "That's nothing! My mother looked back and turned into a telephone pole!"[6]

Some people don't pay attention to how they turn around spiritually either. Their repentance is not genuine. How can we know when someone's repentance is real? In speaking before King Agrippa, Paul gave us the answer: "I preached that they should repent and turn to God and prove their repentance by their deeds" (Acts 26:20). Some people in God's Word demonstrated their real motives by their actions.

Jealous King Saul relentlessly chased after David and attempted to kill him. Ironically, David had the golden opportunity to kill Saul, but he spared the king's life instead. When David made himself known to the king, Saul wept, "You are more righteous than I ... You have treated me well, but I have treated you badly" (1 Samuel 24:17). David gave his oath to Saul that he would not wipe out his descendants as a sign of his forgiveness. But David did not trust Saul, and while the king returned home, David and his men went up to the stronghold. It was a wise decision. Later Saul pursued David all over again.

When Saul was weeping and realizing he was to blame, he had remorse for his sins, but it wasn't enough to make him totally change his ways. Remorse is sorrow for sin. But remorse is not true repentance. It takes more than being sorry to make a u-turned life.

Rather, a godly sorrow leads to repentance. Paul wrote how the Corinthians had this kind of sorrow and what fruits it brought forth: "Godly sorrow brings repentance that leads to salvation and leaves no regret, but worldly sorrow brings death. See what this godly sorrow has produced in you: what earnestness, what eagerness to clear yourselves, what indignation, what alarm, what longing, what concern, what readiness to see justice done" (2 Corinthians 7:10-11).

We see this kind of "readiness to see justice done" in the life of Zacchaeus. Zacchaeus might have been a short man physically, but he was not short on funds. As a tax collector for the Romans, he had grown rich from extorting extra taxes from his fellow Jews, which caused them to despise him. When Jesus came to Zacchaeus' house, this little man showed how big his heart could be when he told Jesus, "Look, Lord! Here and now I give half of my possessions to the poor, and if I have cheated anybody out of anything, I will pay back four times the amount" (Luke 19:8). His changed, u-turned heart manifested itself in a u-turned lifestyle.

Paul and Silas witnessed another u-turned life when they were thrown into a Philippian jail. After being severely flogged, they began praying and singing with the other prisoners as their "captive" audience. Suddenly an earthquake rocked the prison, and the jailer in charge was ready to kill himself because he thought the prisoners had escaped. He asked what he should do and was taught the good news by Paul and Silas. He then washed their wounds and was later baptized with his household. That was quite a change for a toughened Roman jailer (Acts 16:22-34)!

Whose Responsibility?

From the previous examples, we see that only genuine repentance pleases God. When one has truly repented, God will forgive him. There is no question that God requires repentance for us to come to Him. Numerous passages make that very clear (Ezekiel 14:6; 18:30-32; Matthew 3:2; 4:17; Luke 13:3-5; Acts 3:19; 17:30). Most importantly, in order for us to be saved, God's Word tells us to move out in faith to repent, confess our sins, and be baptized for the remission (or forgiveness) of our sins (Acts 2:38).

• *If We Offend.* While God requires repentance in our relationship with Him, what is our responsibility to those we offend? Jesus taught, "Therefore, if you are offering your gift at the altar and there remember that your brother has something against you, leave your gift there in front of the altar. First go and be reconciled to your brother; then come and offer your gift" (Matthew 5:23-24). Jesus was referring to worship in the temple. In Old Testament worship, God would not accept a person's sacrifice if he was not in good standing with his Lord and his neighbor (Isaiah 1:10-17; Amos 5:21-24).[7] Following this principle, we should make amends with those we have offended as soon as we can.

• *If We Are Offended.* What should we do if someone offends us? Again Jesus taught, "So watch yourselves. If your brother sins, rebuke him, and if he repents, forgive him. If he sins against you seven times in a day, and seven times comes back to you and says, 'I repent,' forgive him" (Luke 17:3-4). Here the Lord made the point that no matter how many times someone comes to ask our forgiveness, we must give it. There is no limit making us free of this responsibility.

Some people feel that this verse justifies us to withhold forgiveness until a person asks for it. However, if we look closely, Jesus is emphasizing the responsibility we have (rebuking and forgiving) instead of the absence of our responsibility. Christ did not say we must forgive "if and only if" someone asks our forgiveness. We must not add to God's Word what is not there.[8]

In other scriptures He commanded that we must forgive others or we will not be forgiven ourselves (Matthew 6:12, 14; 18:35). Mark 11:25 makes it clear: "And when you stand praying, if you hold anything against anyone, forgive him, so that your Father in heaven may forgive you your sins." Note the immediate action taken in prayer – forgiving right then and there without waiting on the actions of the offender. Then we stand justified in our prayers before God.

The Scriptures contain several examples of people who freely forgave their offenders before or without repentance. Joseph wept and forgave his brothers when they were still terrified in his presence (Genesis 45:1-15). Moses prayed for the rebellious Israelites to be forgiven when they crafted the golden calf (Exodus 32:31-32). Stephen forgave his killers even as they stoned him (Acts 7:59-60).

Forgiveness Is Our Responsibility

The case of Stephen brings up an important point. Stephen was dying. If he were bound to wait for his killers' repentance, he would not have been able to grant it. If his killers later repented, they could not ask his forgiveness. He would have died unforgiving, and they would have eventually died unforgiven.

Today we face the same dilemma if we feel bound to wait for another's repentance before we can grant forgiveness. What if someone's carelessness causes you serious health problems, but she is totally unaware of what she did? Or what if you cannot contact her? What if a rapist is caught but never sees the need to repent or say, "I'm sorry"? How can the teacher who unmercifully humiliated you years ago apologize when she now has Alzheimer's and doesn't know who she is let alone who you are? What if your father's business partner cheated your family out of thousands of dollars but will not admit his mistake? Or how can a woman widowed by the attacks on Sept. 11, 2001 forgive the hijackers and every other terrorist who was involved when some of them are dead and others she will never see?

Our responsibility to forgive does not depend on the actions of others. Forgiveness is an act of will, something we choose to do, and is independent of the decisions of others. Whatever the circumstance, we have the responsibility to forgive. It brings us one step closer to what we often hope forgiveness will bring – reconciliation.

Stopping to Ask

1. What are some meanings for the original Hebrew and Greek words for repentance?

2. Why did Paul experience such a dramatic transformation in his conversion? Why were the Jews at Damascus baffled at the change?

3. How did Paul describe his life before and after his conversion (Romans 7:24; 1 Timothy 1:16; Ephesians 3:8; 1 Corinthians 15:9-10)?

4. How do Ezekiel 14:6; 18:30; Matthew 3:2; 4:17; Luke 13:3-5; Acts 3:19; 17:30 show that God requires our repentance before we can be acceptable to Him?

5. What is the difference between worldly sorrow and godly sorrow (2 Corinthians 7:10-11)?

6. How did Saul, Zacchaeus and the Philippian jailer show their repentance was genuine?

7. What are the steps we must take to be saved (Mark 16:16; Acts 2:38; Romans 10:9-10, 17; Revelation 14:12-13)?

8. What is our responsibility when we offend another (Matthew 5:23-24)? What is our responsibility when someone offends us (Luke 17:3-4)?

9. What will happen if we refuse to forgive another (Matthew 6:12, 14; 18:35; Mark 11:25)?

10. In the Bible, who forgave others before or without their repentance?

Going Further – Acts 8:9-25

1. What was Simon's occupation? Why did the people follow him? What changed his occupation and his life?

2. What did Peter and John have that Simon was willing to pay for? What did Peter tell Simon to do? Was Simon willing to repent?

3. How can we encourage Christian brothers and sisters who have fallen away to turn back to God?

What If They Just Won't Listen?

Y ou've cried. You've cajoled. You've pleaded. You want to forgive and be reconciled. But still your wayward Christian sister will not listen. Or your erring Christian brother refuses to heed your warning. What should you do?

Jesus addressed this dilemma in Matthew 18:15-17. In the preceding verses he told the parable of the lost sheep, in which the shepherd left the 99 and searched for one wandering sheep. He concluded, "In the same way your Father in heaven is not willing that any of these little ones should be lost" (v. 14). Jesus continued to discuss how to bring back wandering brothers and sisters who won't listen to our pleas to return to the fold. He outlines four stages of concern to help bring them back.

• *Talk Together Privately.* Rebuke is never easy to take, but it can be easier when a caring Christian meets with another one-on-one. Paul echoes this idea in Galatians 6:1: "Brothers, if someone is caught in a sin, you who are spiritual should restore him gently."

• *Take One or Two Witnesses.* If the wanderer still does not listen, then maybe one or two others can say something to convince him to repent. Jesus said, "[E]very matter may be established by the testimony of two or three witnesses" (Matthew 18:16; Deuteronomy 19:15). These witnesses could confirm what was said and done and possibly help change the wanderer's mind.

• *Involve the Church.* If the guilty one will not change, the church as a caring membership must urge the unrepentant to come back, "speaking the truth in love" (Ephesians 4:15).

• *Regard Him as an Outsider.* If all these demonstrations of concern fail and the erring one still will not listen, then he is the one who chooses to leave fellowship with God and the church. He is the one who has already considered himself an outsider. The church only affirms what he has already decided. It is definitely within his power to change, and it is with this in mind that he is excluded in the first place.[9] The whole purpose of disfellowshipping is to bring the wanderer back – from death" (James 5:19-20).

Chapter 11

Patching Things Up

"The most important trip you may take in life is meeting people halfway."
- Henry Boye [1]

If you had the fortune (or misfortune) to travel in a Model T in the 1920s, patching things up was the only way to keep going. There used to be a saying referring to that mode of travel: "If you had a pair of pliers and some bailing wire, you could keep on traveling." [2] You might travel a little farther if you had tools for fixing a flat tire – a jack, a hand pump, and some patching rubber. [3] Flat tires were inevitable, and you had to be prepared for a blowout every 50-100 miles or so. [4]

To fix a flat, you had to take out the tire's inner tube and find the puncture, which you then patched and glued. After the leak was tested, the repaired inner tube was put back inside the tire, which was then put on the rim. The tire was then pumped full of air with a hand pump. Sometimes the whole process took about two hours, and that's if the weather was good. Inclement weather such as snow or rain would hinder your progress. That was quite an operation, especially if you were just out for a Sunday afternoon drive! [5]

Spiritually, patching things up is also the only way to keep on going. It takes more than pliers and bailing wire to keep people together, though. We will have relational blowouts. Keep the patching materials – love and forgiveness – handy for the next time because we will need them. We need to try everything we can to patch things up when people hurt one another.

Patching things up with one another – reconciliation – is the goal of forgiveness. To be reunited with another person is the culmination of forgiveness. However, reconciling is not always the end result when we forgive or are forgiven. It is not always advisable to reconcile with those involved in violent behavior, stalking or sexual abuse. We don't have to beat ourselves emotionally if we cannot reconcile with everyone.[6] Sadly, everyone is not interested in reconciling with us, even if we would do almost anything to accomplish that goal. We can still forgive people without being in a relationship with them.

Even if things seem beyond healing, that does not excuse us from trying to reconcile when our relationships need mending. Whenever possible, God desires for us to patch up our blown out relationships.

A Father and Two Sons

"Dad – give me my inheritance now." This is what a younger son demanded of his father in a parable Jesus told in Luke 15:11-32. His request could have been considered rebellious in that culture and punishable by beating or worse from his father (Deuteronomy 21:18-21). This impatient son, unmarried and therefore presumably not older than 18, would have little experience in handling money.[7] Yet, despite his son's selfishness, the father gave him his share. The son took off to a far country and squandered what he had in wild living.

It did not take long for all his money and friends to disappear. In the midst of a famine and with no resources, he found a job feeding pigs, which Jews were forbidden to do. He was reduced to longing to eat the pods that the pigs were eating because no one offered him anything else.

His gnawing, empty stomach brought to mind better days at home, where even the hired men had plenty to eat. The hired men were the day laborers, the "temps" of that day who could be hired at a moment's notice. They were lower than the family slaves and held no place in the family like slaves did. This is the position that the son thought he might be able to attain since he didn't expect to return as a son. At least as a hired man he would eat. He had his speech prepared and might have been practicing it as he headed toward home.[8]

Unexpected Reception

What happened next was totally unexpected. The son's father caught a glimpse of his son in the distance and his heart filled with compassion. Although he was a man of wealth and property, the father cast aside his dignity and started running! He would have had to pull up his long robes as he ran. He joyfully rushed to welcome his returning son and then threw his arms around him and kissed him.[9]

The son began his speech, but he didn't get a chance to finish. The father interrupted him by commanding his servants to bring the best robe (belonging to the father himself and usually given to a guest of honor), the ring (probably the family ring, signifying authority and reinstatement to the family), and sandals (for a free man because only slaves went barefoot). We don't know, but it is possible that the son still had the stench of pigs on his ragged clothes! Yet his father, by his actions, was saying that he welcomed him as his son.[10, 11]

The fattened calf, which was saved only for special occasions, was killed.[12] Such an offering was probably enough for a party for the whole village.[13] Hearing the sounds of music and dancing, the older brother asked a servant to discover what the celebration was about. When the servant told him, he became angry and refused to go in.

Ironically, it was usually an older brother who settled differences between a father and a younger brother. But here the father came outside from the party to plead with his older son to rejoice with the others that his brother had returned.[14] The brother disrespectfully harangued his father for not giving him even a young goat so that he could celebrate with his friends. He told his father how he had faithfully slaved for him all these years without disobeying him. Then he accused, "But when this son of yours who has squandered your property with prostitutes comes home, you kill the fattened calf for him!" (Luke 15:30). The older son's self-righteousness came spilling out to betray his true feelings.[15]

The father's reply was one of tenderness as it had been with his younger son. The father told the older son everything he had belonged to him. But the father repeated, "But we had to celebrate and be glad, because this brother of yours was dead and is alive again; he was lost and is found" (Luke 15:32).[16]

Jesus did not give His listeners an ending to the story. We are left to wonder if the older brother changed his mind and rejoiced with the family over his newly found brother. We also wonder what our response will be when our brother is lost and then found. Or how will we react when a sister has been overtaken by sin and wants to repent and come back to God? Will the atmosphere be receptive? Will we celebrate and rejoice? Or will we snicker and gossip about what she has done or refuse to welcome her back? It will help us to remember that one day each of us might be the prodigal brother or sister who needs to come back to our Father.

The Climate of Forgiveness

When we are open to each other, we create a climate for forgiveness. This openness involves the same qualities we see in the father of the prodigal son. Throughout the story we see a father who is open to his straying son. First his eyes were open; he seemed to be looking down the road, searching the distant horizon for the figure he longed to see. His heart was also open. He didn't close it to the possibility of reconciliation. Even though his heart was in pain, he kept hoping for his son to return. Finally, his arms were open. When he saw his son, he took off running and embraced his son and kissed him.

Just like the father in the parable, we can create this same climate for forgiveness when we are open. We need intentionally to look for opportunities when someone might be more receptive to reconciliation. We might miss an opportunity if we are not looking for it. We should keep our hearts open to reconciliation as well. And we should be ready with open arms to welcome someone home!

Jesus' parable of the prodigal gives a beautiful portrait of the open and accepting nature of our Father God. As we picture the father in the story running, embracing and kissing his long-lost son, we can see a God who is eager for us to come back to Him when we stray. Dale and Juanita Ryan write, "God's forgiveness is a wild, passionate, unrestrained longing for us, love for us, delight in us, celebration of us, embracing of us as his very own children." [17] Is this not what we see in Jesus' words? "Come to me, all you who are weary and burdened, and I will give you rest. Take my yoke upon you and learn from me, for I am gentle and humble in heart, and you will find rest for your souls. For my yoke is easy and my burden is light" (Matthew 11:28-30).

In Times of Crisis

Keeping a climate open to reconciliation is not always easy, especially in times of crisis. In 1966, in the midst of the Middle East conflict, one priest felt uneasy as he led the service one Sunday. Bitterness hung heavy in the air between the Arab and Jewish converts. Taking an extreme measure, he decided to lock the doors at the end of the service. He then stood up and told the members that Jesus Christ was the only one who could help them in their conflict. They had two choices. Either they could kill each other and he would conduct their funerals without cost, or they could forgive each other and work toward reconciliation and become closer to what God would have them be.

For 10 minutes there was an awkward silence. Finally an Israeli village policeman stood up and said he was willing to forgive everyone in the congregation. He asked that everyone forgive him as well. Then he and the priest embraced. The priest called for everyone else to do the same. It was only a beginning, but it was a breakthrough.[18]

A climate of disharmony and discord reigns in some of our congregations of the Lord's church. Backbiting and hard feelings remain about occurrences that should have been dealt with and long forgotten. Straying members would like to return to God but think they will not be received. What would happen if we were to ask people to consider forgiving and reconciling before they left the service? What if we were to start opening up to others to change the climate to one of forgiveness and reconciliation? What would it be like if we determined to come back to the next meeting, ready to tell how we had tried to make wrongs right by making a visit or a phone call, writing a letter, repaying a debt or otherwise trying to make amends? Reconciling or patching up the world, the church, the home or a relationship begins with each one of us – you and me!

Genuine Reconciliation

Jesus shows us what true reconciliation is – being estranged from God by the depravity of our sins and then brought together with Him by Christ's blood. Paul wrote in Romans 5:6-11:

> You see, at just the right time, when we were still powerless, Christ died for the ungodly. Very rarely will anyone die

for a righteous man, though for a good man someone might possibly dare to die. But God demonstrates his own love for us in this: While we were still sinners, Christ died for us. Since we have now been justified by his blood, how much more shall we be saved from God's wrath through him! For if, when we were God's enemies, we were reconciled to him through the death of his Son, how much more, having been reconciled, shall we be saved through his life! Not only is this so, but we also rejoice in God through our Lord Jesus Christ, through whom we have now received reconciliation.

Stopping to Ask

1. What is the goal of forgiveness? Why is it not always the end result?

2. Why could the younger son in Jesus' parable be considered rebellious and deserving of a beating or worse? Why do you think the father let him have his inheritance anyway?

3. What did the son do with his money? What happened to his money and friends?

4. What job did the son find? What did the boy decide to do?

5. In a family with servants, what was the difference between hired men and slaves?

6. Why was it undignified for the father to run? What else did he do when his son returned? How did he demonstrate to his son that he was welcomed back as a son?

7. Whose job was it to settle differences in the family? Why was this family different?

8. How did the father create an open climate for forgiving his son?

9. How can we create a climate of forgiveness?

10. How is the father in Jesus' parable like our Father God?

Going Further –
Galatians 3:27; 2 Corinthians 5:17-21

1. How does a person get into Christ? If a person is in Christ, what kind of creature is he or she?

2. God brought us back – reconciled us – to Him through whom? In reconciliation, what did God not count against us?

3. What is the message of reconciliation? When God makes His appeal through us, what do we become?

4. Christ was without sin, but what did He become for us? What does Christ's role in reconciliation mean to you personally?

Does God Really Forget Our Sins?

When He forgives us our sins, how then can an omnipresent, omniscient and omnipotent God forget them? When He wipes our slate clean, does He also obliterate our sins from His memory and develop a case of "holy amnesia"? Some scriptures seem to indicate that. In Jeremiah 31:34b, God declares, "For I will forgive their wickedness and will remember their sins no more." Again in Isaiah 43:25, He proclaims, "I, even I, am he who blots out your transgressions, for my own sake, and remembers your sins no more."

Yet how can God judge us if He has only a record of our good deeds and none of our bad? Paul states in 2 Corinthians 5:10: "For we must all appear before the judgment seat of Christ, that each one may receive what is due him for the things done while in the body, whether good or bad." Certainly God will need a memory or record of all our actions to determine our eternal destiny and our reward.[19]

Ezekiel uses an expression that makes God's remembrance of sins easier to understand. In speaking of the evil man who repents, Ezekiel 33:16 states, "None of the sins he has committed will be remembered against him. He has done what is just and right; he will surely live." The same expression is used in a similar passage in 18:22. And David says it in yet another way: "Blessed is the man whose sin the Lord does not count against him" (Psalm 32:2). The point is that when God forgives us, He will not use those sins against us later. Those sins aren't brought up to haunt us in the future.

It is interesting that the writer of Hebrews repeats portions of Jeremiah 31:34 twice (Hebrews 8:12; 10:17). In this context the writer of Hebrews is speaking about the blessings of the new covenant. As Christians in that covenant, our sins have been dealt with by Jesus' sacrifice and God does not choose to remember them. We can be truly forgiven, and He won't count our sins against us ever again.

Chapter 12

Restoring Something Worth Saving

*"Forgiveness is not probation; it is restoration –
and that should lead to rejoicing!"* [1]

It was driven out of the showroom shiny and new. But that was years ago. Rusty fenders, rotting seats and worn-out brakes are all that's left. It was abandoned in the salvage yard with the rest of the wrecks.

But someone who thought it was something worth saving saw it. He knew he could restore it to something as good as new. He paid the price and took it home to his garage. Poring over antique automobile catalogs and surfing the Internet, he found just the right parts to take the place of the old ones. After months of painstaking fitting and sanding, molding and painting, it was finished. Under the expert's hand, it was restored to its former glory, and it was a beauty!

Just like that old car, the ravages of sin have wrecked us all. We all need some "body work," specifically in our hearts. God came along and thought we were worth saving. With His expert hand, He can smooth out our rough imperfections and add what we need. God can restore us!

God's restoration of sinful man – this theme takes a deeply personal strain in Psalm 51 where the psalmist wrote, "Restore to me the joy of your salvation and grant me a willing spirit to sustain me" (v. 12). King David is credited for putting his thoughts together so beautifully in this psalm. It was supposedly written after the prophet Nathan accused David of sin, saying point-blank, "You are the man!" (2 Samuel 12:7). What had David done to deserve such a rebuke?

David's Heart Trouble

David was handpicked by God to rule the kingdom of Israel because he was "a man after [God's] own heart" (1 Samuel 13:14). But like all of us, sometimes he had heart trouble. From the palace rooftop one day, he saw a beautiful woman bathing, and his heart was led away (2 Samuel 11:2). He wanted her for himself. Exercising what he thought was his kingly prerogative, he commanded Bathsheba to come to the palace. She became pregnant after their encounter. David called her husband, Uriah, home from battle and encouraged him to sleep with his wife, even getting him drunk, but he refused out of loyalty to his troops. Then the king stooped to murder, commanding that Uriah be left dangerously exposed in battle. After Uriah was killed by the Ammonites in battle, David married Bathsheba as quickly as propriety allowed. He thought his treachery was hidden, but the Lord knew his sins and his heart condition.

That walk on the roof led David down the road of many sins – lust, adultery, lying, murder and stealing – but at the root of all these was his heart problem of ingratitude. God had given him many blessings, but David thought he had to go after another man's wife. It was this ingratitude that Nathan the prophet illustrated so vividly in his parable about the pet lamb. A rich farmer, who had many flocks, confiscated the cherished lamb of a poor farmer. In response to Nathan's story, David indignantly but unknowingly pronounced judgment on himself – the king with several wives who confiscated Uriah's wife. [2]

In his mind, David probably justified his actions with thoughts like ...

"I'm king of the nation. It's okay to have any woman I want."

"It was only one rendezvous, and it's okay because she is married and not a virgin."

"She is married, so it's okay if she has a child."

"It's okay if Uriah gets killed. After all, he's a soldier. Soldiers die all the time."

But David found he could not justify the secret guilt that was gnawing at his heart. Only God could take away David's guilt. He is the only one who can take away our guilt as well. A closer look at Psalm 51 will help us understand how God deals with guilt and sin and how He can restore us just as He restored David.

A One-Sided Love Triangle

Novelists weave their stories about love triangles where two lovers plan the death of an unfortunate husband or wife. But David's case was no two-sided plot. The king knew he was the one at fault. He was the mastermind of this sordid affair. He also knew that ultimately his sin was against God. So he wrote, "For I know my transgressions, and my sin is always before me. Against you, you only, have I sinned and done what is evil in your sight, so that you are proved right when you speak and justified when you judge" (Psalm 51:3-4). True, he had sinned against Uriah, Bathsheba, Joab and other innocent soldiers for involving them in the cover-up and intrigue. He may have even sinned against his family and the nation he ruled. But all sin is rebellion against God. David's sin was personally against God because David had despised and disregarded His law. In the same way, when we sin, no matter who is affected, ultimately we sin against God.

David wrote, "Have mercy on me, O God, according to your un-failing love; ... You do not delight in sacrifice, or I would bring it; you do not take pleasure in burnt offerings. The sacrifices of God are a bro-ken spirit; a broken and contrite heart, O God, you will not despise" (Psalm 51:1, 16-17) That doesn't mean God would not honor David's sacrifice. It means the attitude of David's heart meant more than a mere offering. God looks for humble and contrite hearts in us as well before God grants His pardon.

David used three expressions to show what God does to our sins. First he wrote, "[A]ccording to your great compassion blot out my transgressions. ... Hide your face from my sins and blot out all my in-iquity" (Psalm 51:1, 9). Blotting out involved "wiping off" as in a book (Exodus 32:32; Nehemiah 13:14) or water on a dish (2 Kings 21:13). [3,4] David asked that his sins be wiped off and removed so he wouldn't have to see them anymore.

Second, he pleaded, "Wash away all my iniquity ... wash me, and I will be whiter than snow" (Psalm 51:2, 7). Washing here actually was a launderer's term, which meant more than a quick dip and rinse. This was more like a "power wash," washing vigorously by stamping, rub-bing, even pounding to loosen the dirt. [5] David saw sin so set in the fab-ric of his life that only God's thorough intensive stain treatment would do.[6] Only God could get it "whiter than snow."

Third, David requested, "[C]leanse me from my sin. ... Cleanse me with hyssop, and I will be clean" (Psalm 51:2, 7). According to the Law this cleansing referred to the ceremonial washing that declared a leper healed (Leviticus 14:8-9) and a man purified after touching a dead body (Numbers 19:18).[7] After this ritual a person presented himself to the priest. If the priest was satisfied that all the requirements had been met, then he sprinkled the person with water and a bunch of hyssop. This was a symbolic cleansing that would put the person in fellowship with God and the Jewish community again. David hoped God would declare him cleansed from all sin and in fellowship with him.[8]

God can do the same for us. He can wipe our sins away so that they are out of sight. He can cleanse us from the dreaded defilement of sin to put us in fellowship with Him and our brothers and sisters in Christ (1 John 1:6-7). He can give us a hand-rubbing, stone-pounding, foot stomping "power wash" to get us whiter than snow!

In Psalm 51 David makes an amazing request: to receive a totally new heart. "Create in me a pure heart, O God, and renew a steadfast spirit within me" (v. 10). The Hebrew word for "create" is the same one used in Genesis 1:1, which states God created the heavens and the earth. David asked that God let him start over with a new heart, complete with a fresh outlook in his choices, thoughts, attitudes and motivation.[9] We could certainly use a fresh start whenever we sin!

David then speaks about the joy he felt when in fellowship with God and longs for it again. "Restore to me the joy of your salvation and grant me a willing spirit, to sustain me" (Psalm 51:12). This restoration and forgiveness were granted him when he admitted his sins to Nathan. "Then David said to Nathan, 'I have sinned against the Lord.' Nathan replied, 'The Lord has taken away your sin. You are not going to die. But because by doing this you have made the enemies of the Lord show utter contempt, the son born to you will die' " (2 Samuel 12:13-14). Although David was forgiven, he still had to bear the earthly consequences of sin. But he could look back and know that God would restore their relationship. The Lord could pardon him from his past for a much better future. Though God will forgive us if we repent, we must still bear the consequences of our sins, but we, as David, can know He will restore us too.

Before and After Pictures

Sometimes when someone restores an old car, he will take pictures of the dents, the rusting fender, and the ragged seat covers. He wants to remember how much better the restoration looks compared to the car's former condition. He doesn't dwell on the old but delights in the new. The old is a point of comparison, a point of departure. After all, you don't know how far you've come unless you know where you've been.

The same was true for David. He knew about his affair with Bathsheba and wanted to remember how far he had come. In a sense he developed his "before" and "after" pictures in Psalm 32. In this psalm attributed to David, he rejoiced that his sins were forgiven, at the same time remembering how he suffered when he tried to hide them. Some commentators think that this psalm was written after Psalm 51, when David had had time to think about his experience and could instruct others to learn from it. In the beginning of the psalm (32:1-7), David wrote:

> Blessed is he whose transgressions are forgiven, whose sins are covered. Blessed is the man whose sin the Lord does not count against him and in whose spirit is no deceit. When I kept silent, my bones wasted away through my groaning all day long. For day and night your hand was heavy upon me; my strength was sapped as in the heat of summer. Then I acknowledged my sin to you and did not cover up my iniquity. I said, "I will confess my transgressions to the Lord" – and you forgave the guilt of my sin. Therefore let everyone who is godly pray to you while you may be found; surely when the mighty waters rise, they will not reach him. You are my hiding place; you will protect me from trouble and surround me with songs of deliverance.

Our lives can be songs of praise of deliverance to God for His forgiveness and pardon. Just like David, we can remember the "befores" of sin and guilt to appreciate the "afters" in our lives. He can restore us as He restored David.

The Joy of Restoration

Few scenes of restoration in the Bible are more poignant than that of the sinful woman who found forgiveness in Jesus (Luke 7:36-50). She was probably a prostitute, but Jesus saw someone worth saving. Her faith and love spilled over in gratitude. To show how much she cared, she bravely entered Simon the Pharisee's house where Jesus had been invited for dinner. Even though anyone could come and watch on such an occasion, she might have encountered looks of condemnation from the guests. Probably thinking of her past life, she was overcome and started to weep.[10] As her tears fell on Jesus' feet, she wiped them with her hair, continually kissed them, and anointed them with perfume.[11]

This display of appreciation for Jesus was lost on Simon. He could only think how the Lord must not be a prophet or He would have realized what kind of immoral woman was touching Him. Little did Simon know that not only did Jesus know her past, but He also knew Simon's very thoughts! [12]

Jesus told Simon a parable about two debtors who owed a moneylender 50 denarii and 500 denarii. Because a denarius was about a day's wage, the debts amounted to 50 days' wage versus 1⅓ years' salary – quite a difference! [13] Neither man could repay, so the moneylender forgave them their debts. Jesus asked Simon which debtor loved the lender more. Simon admitted it was the one who had owed more.

Then Jesus brought the point of the story home. He reminded the Pharisee that he had not bothered to provide the basic courtesies to welcome Him as a guest – kissing Him, washing His dusty feet, and anointing His head with oil. These were provided instead by a sinful woman in her own way. Jesus concluded, "[H]er many sins have been forgiven – for she loved much. But he who has been forgiven little loves little" (Luke 7:47). The joy of her forgiveness was displayed in humble service and loving gratitude.[14] After Jesus forgave her sins, He pronounced that her faith had saved her. Jesus said something to her that is easy to miss – "Go in peace" (literally "Go into peace"). Jesus bade her farewell with the hope that her new life would be one of restoration and peace.[15]

"It's Me, Oh Lord"

How often are we like Simon, criticizing others for their faults when we have bigger problems ourselves? Do we have a hard time seeing the speck of dirt in our brother or sister's eye because we have a big beam of lumber in our own? We need to remember the lyrics of the old spiritual, "It's not my brother nor my sister, but it's me, oh Lord, standin' in the need of prayer." Or do we have the courage of that sinful woman to admit our sin before others? Do we have the joy she had in her salvation when she repented and obeyed the Lord? Do we have the overwhelming gratitude spilling over to show our Lord how thankful we are? May we pray like David, "Restore to me the joy of your salvation."

Stopping to Ask

1. How is David described in 1 Samuel 13:14? How did he allow his heart to be led away (2 Samuel 11:2)?

2. What was David's intention when he commanded Uriah to come home? What foiled David's plan? What did he finally resort to?

3. What sins did David commit in his affair with Bathsheba?

4. What was at the root of David's heart problem? How is this demonstrated in Nathan's parable?

5. Whom was David's sin ultimately against? Who was affected by his sins?

6. Did the Old Testament Law make provisions for sacrifice for murder and adultery? Why do you think David was not punished according to the Law?

7. In Psalm 51 what did David mean by the following expressions: blotting out, washing, cleansing?

8. What other scripture mentioned in the chapter has the same word and meaning as "create" in Psalm 51:10?

9. What was the consequence of David's sin? How did he describe the "before" and "after" of his sins in Psalm 32?

10. How could you contrast the attitudes of Simon and the sinful woman? How did Jesus contrast the two debtors in His parable? How did He relate His parable to Simon and the sinful woman?

Going Further – Daniel 4

1. Describe Nebuchadnezzar's dream about a tree. Who was not able to interpret it? Who finally interpreted it?

2. Why did the dream perplex Daniel? What was the interpretation?

3. What happened to Nebuchadnezzar 12 months later? Why was he eventually restored to his kingdom?

4. If God was willing to restore an evil king when he repented, is He less willing to restore us today?

Was There Complete Forgiveness in the Old Testament?

D avid's sin with Bathsheba spiraled into multiple sins and a myriad of consequences. But just like others who repented of their sins in the Old Testament, David experienced the forgiveness of God (Psalm 32:5). That forgiveness was real, but it was incomplete. Old Testament sacrifices had to be made repeatedly because they were not adequate to remove sin entirely. Only Christ, the Perfect Sacrifice, was sufficient to provide total forgiveness. Only He "died as a ransom to set them free from the sins committed under the first covenant" (Hebrews 9:15).

The writer of Hebrews says it best:

> The law is only a shadow of the good things that are coming – not the realities themselves. For this reason it can never, by the same sacrifices repeated endlessly year after year, make perfect those who draw near to worship. If it could, would they not have stopped being offered? For the worshipers would have been cleansed once for all, and would no longer have felt guilty for their sins. But those sacrifices are an annual reminder of sins, because it is impossible for the blood of bulls and goats to take away sins. (Hebrews 10:1-4)

Priests of the Old Law offered various sacrifices – burnt offerings, grain offerings, drink offerings, meat offerings of the High Priest, as well as the offerings of incense (Exodus 30:7-8; Leviticus 6:8-23; Numbers 28:3-8). William Barclay wrote describing these: "There was a kind of priestly treadmill of sacrifice. Moffatt speaks of 'the levitical drudges' who day in day out, kept offering these sacrifices. There was no end to this process and it left men still conscious of their sin." [16]

The Hebrews writer makes an interesting contrast between the postures of the Levitical priests and Christ in Hebrews 10:11-12. Old Testament priests had to stand during all their never-ending sacrificial work. But Christ, our High Priest, is now sitting at the right hand of God. Not only is Christ's atoning work finished, but He also is exalted in a place of honor and glory (Hebrews 10:14, 18). [17]

Chapter 13

The Last Few Miles

*"Forgiveness has many layers, many seasons ...
The important part of forgiveness is to begin and
to continue. The finishing of it all is a life work."*
~ Clarissa Pinkola Estes [1]

A nyone who has ever traveled with small children knows how difficult the last few miles of the trip can be. Often those miles seem the longest and the hardest. Even if the road is as flat as a pancake, it becomes an uphill journey. Games of "I spy" or "Count the license plates" can only last for so long. When everyone is the tiredest and the grumpiest, fears need to be calmed ("What will it be like?") and excitement channeled ("I can't wait much longer!"). Undoubtedly toward the end of the day, you hear for the umpteenth time, "Are we there yet?"

When our children would ask that question on our family trips, my husband and I would reply something like, "We're getting closer all the time." Knowing our destination was getting closer would usually satisfy their curiosity and give us peace for about five more minutes.

It's the same with our journey to forgiveness. With any progress toward forgiving someone else, we are closer to forgiveness than before. Perhaps there are no quantum leaps, but that is not what is important. The goal of forgiveness becomes clearer with each mile we go. The last few miles become bearable because the end of the journey is in sight. Those seemingly never-ending miles might hold the culmination of all our efforts so we must not give up. And the results might reach further than we could imagine.

A Journey's Surprise Ending

Jacob was scared – and he had reason to be. This Old Testament patriarch literally thought he might be traveling the last few miles to his death. He was going home, and his brother Esau was coming to meet him with 400 men. Somehow it didn't seem like a welcoming party. Jacob might have envisioned an army of armed and dangerous vigilantes bent on revenge. Fearing for his life and his family, he divided his large entourage into two groups so that if one group was attacked, the other one could escape. He also handpicked a generous gift of livestock to go in front of the group to appease his brother (Genesis 32:1-8, 13-16).

Jacob's mind probably went back to his younger years at home with his parents, Isaac and Rebekah. Esau was his twin brother, but the similarities ended there. The favorite of his father, Esau was hairy and red (Esau's name meant "red"). He liked to hunt and roam outdoors. Jacob, on the other hand, was Rebekah's favorite. He was a homebody, tending his flocks and preparing tasty dishes. One of these dishes, lentils, was so appealing to the famished Esau that Esau traded it for his birthright with all its rights and privileges. Esau was foolish to agree to such a deal, but the conniving Jacob lived up to what his name meant – "deceiver." Later Jacob, with the help of Rebekah, deceived Isaac into giving Jacob his father's blessing. Esau was enraged and vowed to kill Jacob after their father died.

That's why Jacob was scared. He knew his actions had been despicable and dishonest. He had been a liar and a cheat. What would Esau do to him? What would he do to his family?

Years of living on the edge had taught Jacob that he needed something more than himself in situations like these – he needed God. He prayed that God would deliver him and his family. He woke up the next morning, ready for the worst.

Jacob didn't know what to expect, but he probably didn't imagine what happened next. Jacob looked up and saw his brother with his 400 men. As they approached, Jacob bowed to the ground seven times before Esau. "But Esau ran to meet Jacob and embraced him; he threw his arms around his neck and kissed him. And they wept" (Genesis 33:4). Years of rage and fear were washed away. The hugs, the tears, the immense relief, the overwhelming joy – these must have permeated the whole entourage. That day two families became one. Hate and bitterness were lost in joy and reconciliation.

This scene could not have been lost on the family of Jacob and the men of Esau. Think what effect this must have had, especially on the young Joseph. We don't know exactly what age he was, but he was old enough to bow with his mother, Rachel (Genesis 33:7). He might have been old enough to remember the tense anticipation and the subsequent release of years of emotions. The tears, the embraces, the words of forgiveness must have left an indelible stamp on his senses.

The events of this day were probably rehearsed throughout Joseph's youth. There is no way to know their full effect on following generations. Who knows what an impression this reconciliation might have had on him when, years later, Joseph reconciled with his own brothers? What a difference it might have made in his family as this story was passed down from fathers to sons in the years to come.

Making Forgiveness Real for Future Generations

Jacob's and Joseph's stories of forgiveness continue to touch us even today. Stories like theirs in God's Word can give us all examples of how we should forgive. If we follow those examples, just think how forgiveness in our own lives could touch others now and in the future.

For example, we can never know how an impressionable child will be influenced for good. The forgiveness exemplified by Jacob and Esau may have affected generations through Joseph; what better way is there to teach children the blessings of forgiveness than to model it ourselves? Whether they are children around our family table, on a school sports team, in our neighborhood play group, or in our church classroom, our actions speak louder than our words. If we daily show what it means to forgive, then the children we know will more likely emulate it in their own lives.

We should try to take the time to understand what children perceive about forgiveness. By working with their misconceptions and encouraging their questions, we can better ascertain how they feel. Encountering situations in which someone is unfair to them can generate discussion about what they should do next. We should be careful, however, not to "preach" forgiveness or they will dread telling us about their day. We can try to bring it up naturally when it is appropriate, posing questions like: Have you thought about forgiving him or her? What might happen if you did? If the person doesn't apologize, are you still going to forgive? Would you still forgive if your friends didn't want you to? What would Jesus do in your situation? [2]

Sharing stories from books and movies creates another avenue to teach young people values, especially about forgiveness. Stories can show what forgiveness is, how it is rewarded, and how the alternatives – bitterness and revenge – are eventually punished. Some stories, like *The Giving Tree* and Dr. Seuss' *Horton Hears a Who*, teach qualities such as respect, love and generosity that can lead to forgiveness. In *Lilly's Purple Plastic Purse*, younger children can learn what they can do to make amends after someone has tried to get even. Despite its title, *The Hating Book* shows how friends can reconcile after a misunderstanding. For older readers, *The Bronze Bow* depicts a young man's dilemma of whether to choose revenge or forgiveness for the Romans after he hears the teachings of Jesus.

Teenagers, perhaps more resistant to direct teaching, can gain insight from discussing principles of forgiveness and revenge as depicted in novels and movies. Reading class assignments or watching movies together can help open up discussions on characters' motives and reactions. Prime for such discussions are classic novels like *Great Expectations* and *Les Miserables* and movies like *October Sky* and *A Walk to Remember*. [3] Listening and discussing young people's ideas about forgiveness can go a long way toward helping them understand what true forgiveness is.

A Forgiving World Begins With Me

We know that hate and unforgiveness are dangerous to our health. Have you thought about how they affect your family? If these vices are left unchecked, their effects won't stop within your walls. The consequences of their poison can spread outwardly to the church, your community, your town and your nation. They can affect your world.

In contrast, think how forgiveness can affect your neighbor – on the other side of the street and the other side of the world. Even one act of forgiveness can affect generations to come. Forgiveness in one nation can also have global implications. Beginning with a rippling wave, the positive results can produce a flood of goodwill and blessing for many different peoples of the world. [4]

Forgiveness can promote healing and reconciliation in entire nations – one family at a time. Take the country of South Africa. After years of struggle and violence during apartheid, the separatist regime was replaced with a multiracial democracy. To deal with the horrific consequences of those bloody years, the Truth and Reconciliation amnesty hearings were set up. Their purpose was to hear the truth and, if possible, bring about reconciliation between warring factions. Both sides had been guilty of wrongdoing. It was time to try to understand why and stop the violence.

When one of the commissioners asked for further testimony, one young man raised his hand. He addressed the murderers of his father, a despotic chief who had ordered his own people killed. The son admitted initially he had wanted death for his father's killers. After hearing the terrible crimes that his father had committed and how much the people had endured, he better understood why they acted as they did. He asked them to forgive his father and his family. He then in turn offered forgiveness to them. Instead of inciting further violence and hate, he offered forgiveness. The healing could begin for one – then another – and then another. [5]

How Will We Remember?

With all its blessings, however, forgiveness can be risky. You may forgive little wrongs in the family, but forgiving big wrongs between ethnic groups and nations is an immensely difficult order. The enormity of the pain runs too deep and the wounds seemingly will never heal. You cannot be flippant about atrocities committed against an entire country.

People might say, "We can never forgive because we will never forget what they did to us." "They" might mean the Nazis during the holocaust. Or "they" might refer to Pol Pot and his "killing fields" regime in Cambodia or Uganda's brutal president Idi Amin. Or getting closer to home, "they" could mean the terrorists who attacked the World Trade Center on Sept. 11, 2001.

Lewis Smedes writes about the effects of forgiving and forgetting:

> The risks of forgetting are both personal and global. Once we forgive and learn to swallow history's stinking garbage without throwing up, we condition ourselves to digest the worst the monsters of the future can force down our throats. When forgiveness cures our nausea it encourages us to forget that the evil thing happened and can happen again. ... One way to reduce the risk is simply to determine not to let the future generations forget.
>
> We must know, however, that remembering has problems of its own. If forgetting invites repetition, remembering incites perpetuation. Memory can nurse a flame that brings hate to its boiling point, creating a pressure inside that only getting even can relieve. But you cannot get even, not ever, not if you try for a million years. So remembering takes its worst toll on the spirits of the people who suffered most. [6]

Redemptive Remembering

Smedes offers an alternative – redemptive remembering. Who had a more remembering lifestyle than the ancient Hebrews? Smedes relates how God, through Moses, urged the Israelites not only to remember their past but also to teach it to their children and grandchildren so that future generations would not forget. "Only be careful, and watch yourselves closely so that you do not forget the things your eyes have seen or let them slip from your heart as long as you live. Teach them to your children and to their children after them" (Deuteronomy 4:9).

But what were they to remember? Was it the horrors of their slavery or the injustice of Pharaoh or how they had been mistreated for more than 400 years in Egypt? They were urged to remember the miracle of their survival and how God had brought about their salvation. Remembering the past helped them know how far they had come and who they really were. It gave them their identity. The Lord said, "This is a day you are to commemorate; for the generations to come you shall celebrate it as a festival to the Lord – a lasting ordinance. ... And when your children ask you, 'What does this ceremony mean to you?' then tell them, 'It is the Passover sacrifice to the Lord, who passed over the houses of the Israelites in Egypt and spared our homes when he struck down the Egyptians' " (Exodus 12:14, 26-27).

Rather than being bound by the horrors of the past, they were to build their future from learning from the past. Because they were foreigners in a strange land, they were to be hospitable to foreigners in their land (Deuteronomy 24:17-18). Because they had been treated unjustly by harsh taskmasters, they were not to exploit their own poor (vv. 19-22). Because they were once slaves, they were to set their slaves free (15:12-18).[7]

The same is true for us today. As Smedes writes, "Redemptive remembering drives us to a better future, it does not nail us to a worse past."[8] Christians are commanded to remember the cruel death of our Lord as He bore the horrors of a Roman crucifixion. By partaking of the Lord's Supper, we remember how Jesus' body was broken for us and how His blood was shed for us (Luke 22:14-20). But we are not to stop at the inhumanity of such a crime or remember only with resentment that such a thing could happen. Rather we remember that through Christ's death, we have the hope of a resurrection like His (Romans 6:5-10).

As our Father, God has given us the supreme example of forgiveness for the last few miles of our personal journeys. In remembrance of what Jesus did to make it possible for God to forgive us, how can we refuse to forgive? It might be difficult and complicated, but it will also be rewarding, rejuvenating and liberating. So whatever the pain or offense, let us go on and head toward forgiveness. The best way is just to begin!

Stopping to Ask

1. Who was older – Jacob or Esau? What was unusual and prophetic about their activity in Rebekah's womb (Genesis 25:22-24)?

2. What did the twin's names mean? What did they like to do? What bearing could this have had on which parent favored which son?

3. What caused the rift in Jacob and Esau's relationship?

4. Why was Jacob afraid?

5. What happened at Jacob and Esau's meeting? How could this have made an impression on Joseph when in later years he forgave his own brothers?

6. How do our attitudes and actions regarding forgiveness influence the children in our families, church and community?

7. How can forgiveness be considered risky? What are the risks of forgetting and remembering the pain of the past?

8. What does redemptive remembering refer to? How is the Lord's Supper redemptive remembering?

9. What is the most effective, personal way to show children how to forgive?

10. What are some other ways we can teach our children the blessings of forgiveness?

Going Further – Jonah 3:1-10

1. To what city did Jonah preach and why? What was the response of the people there? What is amazing about the response and decree of the king?

2. What did wearing sackcloth signify? Why do you think the king decreed that animals should fast and wear sackcloth too?

3. How did God respond to their repentance? How might the peoples' actions have influenced the king? How might the king's actions serve as a good example to the people?

4. How can our deeds of repentance serve to influence the lives of others?

How Do I Know If I Have Truly Forgiven Someone?

Have you ever been somewhere, but you're not sure you had arrived? The signs said you were there, but nothing looked like you imagined it. You wondered if you had really made it after all.

Often we have the same idea about arriving at forgiveness. How do we know for certain we have arrived? Do feelings of doubt or recurrences of ill-will mean we have not truly forgiven someone else?

It helps to remember that getting to forgiveness is a process, a journey. While total forgiveness without resentment and bitterness is the goal, it might take a while to get there. Each step toward that goal is worthwhile. One day we might make great strides toward our goal. The next day we feel like we are backtracking. We need to be patient with ourselves if we feel like we are not progressing quickly enough. Forgiving can be a long process. [9]

Some questions might help us evaluate how we are moving along to our destination of forgiveness. We can ask: Have I truly committed to forgive? Have I stopped brooding over the offense? Am I trying to understand why the person did what he or she did? Can I see the person as a human being? Do I wish the person well? Do I pray for him or her? If you can do any or all of these things, you are on your way to forgiveness. [10]

Author Clarissa Pinkola Estes gives us some insights to help us know if we have forgiven. She writes:

> You tend to feel sorrow over the circumstances instead of rage, you tend to feel sorry for the person rather than angry with him. You tend to have nothing left to remember to say about it all. You understand the suffering that drove the offense to begin with. You prefer to remain outside the milieu. You are not waiting for anything. You are not wanting anything. There is no lariat snare around your ankle stretching from way back there to here. You are free to go. It may not have turned out to be a happily ever after, but most certainly there is now a fresh Once upon a time waiting for you from this day forward. [11]

A Prayer of Forgiveness

Since ancient times no one has heard,
    no ear has perceived,
no eye has seen any God besides you,
    who acts on behalf of those who wait for him.
You come to the help of those who gladly do right,
    who remember your ways.
But when we continued to sin against them,
    you were angry.
    How then can we be saved?
All of us have become like one who is unclean,
    and all our righteous acts are like filthy rags;
we all shrivel up like a leaf,
    and like the wind our sins sweep us away.
No one calls on your name
    or strives to lay hold of you;
for you have hidden your face from us
    and made us waste away because of our sins.
Yet, O Lord, you are our Father.
    We are the clay, you are the potter;
    we are all the work of your hand.
Do not be angry beyond measure, O Lord;
    do not remember our sins forever.
Oh, look upon us, we pray,
    for we are all your people.

                              Isaiah 64:4-9

Endnotes

Part One – Choosing the Best Route

1. Carrie St. Michael, "Map Attack! We Road Test Online Services," *Good Housekeeping* April 2003: 66.

Chapter 1 – Which Way Is Forgiveness?

1. Don Colbert, *Deadly Emotions: Understand the Mind-Body-Spirit Connection That Can Heal or Destroy You* (Nashville: Thomas Nelson, 2003) 163.

2. Marilyn Meberg, *I'd Rather Be Laughing: Finding Cheer in Every Circumstance* (Nashville: Word, 1998) 123.

3. Robert Jeffress, *When Forgiveness Doesn't Make Sense* (Colorado Springs: WaterBrook Press, 2000) 102-103.

4. Lewis B. Smedes, *Forgive and Forget: Healing the Hurts We Don't Deserve* (New York: HarperSanFrancisco, 1996) 40.

5. Smedes 44-45.

6. Colbert 164-165.

7. Smedes 38-39.

8. Jeffress 47.

9. Jeffress 47.

10. Jeffress 49.

11. Jeffress 51-52.

12. Jeffress 52-54.

13. Jeffress 53.

14. Jeffress 54-55.

15. Craig S. Keener, *The IVP Bible Background Commentary: New Testament* (Downers Grove, Ill.: InterVarsity Press, 1993) 96.

16. Frederick Buechner, *Wishful Thinking: A Seeker's ABC* (1973; San Francisco: Harper San Francisco, 1993) 2.

17. Jeffress 57-58.

18. Robert D. Enright, *Forgiveness Is a Choice: A Step-by-Step Process for Resolving Anger and Restoring Hope* (Washington, D.C.: American Psychological Association, 2001) 239-240.

19. Enright 39.

Chapter 2 – Preparing for the Trip

1. "Forgiveness From *The Joyful Christian*," 6 Oct 2005 <http://www.wildershow.com/cs-lewis-forgive.htm>.

2. Enright 74.

3. David Augsburger, *Caring Enough to Forgive: True Forgiveness* (Ventura, CA: Regal Books, 1981) 62.

4. Andrew J. Weaver and Monica Furlong, eds., *Reflections on Forgiveness and Spiritual Growth* (Nashville: Abingdon Press, 2000) 23.

5. Augsburger 51.

6. Martha Alken, *The Healing Power of Forgiving* (New York: Crossroad Publishing, 1997) 4.

7. Augsburger 12-13.

8. Enright 73.

9. Michael E. McCullough, Steven J. Sandage, and Everett L. Worthington, *To Forgive is Human: How to Put Your Past in the Past* (Downers Grove, Ill.: InterVarsity Press, 1997) 229.

10. Everett Worthington, *Five Steps to Forgiveness: The Art and Science of Forgiving* (New York: Crown Publishers, 2001) 100.

11. McCullough, Sandage and Worthington 229.

12. Colbert 166.

13. Colbert 163.

14. Herbert Lockyer, *All the Men of the Bible* (Grand Rapids: Zondervan, 1958) 227.

Chapter 3 – Following the Signs

1. Michael Youssef, *The Leadership Style of Jesus* (Wheaton: Victor Books, 1986) 83.

2. J.C. Moyer, "Lamb," *The International Standard Bible Encyclopedia*, vol. 3 (Grand Rapids: Eerdmans, 1986) 62.

3. William Barclay, *Jesus as They Saw Him* (Grand Rapids: Eerdmans, 1990) 303-304.

4. Barclay, *Jesus* 306-307.

5. Barclay, *Jesus* 305-306.

6. Barclay, *Jesus* 307.

7. Cornwall 127.

8. Cornwall 127-128.

9. Cornwall 131.

10. James R. Bjorge, *Living in the Forgiveness of God* (Minneapolis: Augsburg, 1990) 13.

11. Jeffress 33-35.

12. Kenneth L. Barker and John Kohlenberger III. *Zondervan NIV Bible Commentary, Vol. 2 New Testament* (Grand Rapids: Zondervan, 1994) 305.

13. Nick Hamilton, "Forgiveness is Better," *Gospel Advocate* June 2002: 20-21.

14. Joy Haney, *How to Forgive When You Don't Feel Like It* (Green Forest, AR: New Leaf Press, 1996) 46.

Chapter 4 – Beyond Road Rage

1. Johann Christoph Arnold, *Why Forgive?* (Farmington, PA: Plough Publishing, 2000) 1.

2. Jeffress 11.

3. L.D. Hatfield, *The True Story of the Hatfield and McCoy Feud* (Charleston, WV: Jarrett Printing, 1944) 46.

4. John T. Willis, *Genesis* (Abilene: ACU Press, 1984) 366-367.

5. Joan Comay and Ronald Brownrigg, *Who's Who in the Bible: Two Volumes in One* (New York, Wings Books, 1980) 48, 207-208.

6. Smedes 131.

7. William Barclay, *The Gospel of Matthew,* vol. 1 (Philadelphia: Westminster Press, 1975) 163.

8. Jack P. Lewis, *The Gospel According to Matthew, Part 1, 1:1-13:52* (Abilene, Texas: ACU Press, 1984) 94.

9. Barclay, *Matthew* 163-164.

10. F.F. Bruce, ed., *The International Bible Commentary* (Grand Rapids: Marshall Pickering/Zondervan, 1986) 1125-1126.

11. Barclay, *Matthew* 165.

12. Barclay, *Matthew* 165.

13. Madeleine S. Miller and J. Lane Miller, *Harper's Bible Dictionary* (New York: Harper & Row, 1973) 53.

14. Leon Morris, *The Gospel According to St. Luke* (Grand Rapids: Eerdmans, 1975) 118.

Chapter 5 – Going Beyond the Expected

1. John Ensor, *Experiencing God's Forgiveness: The Journey From Guilt to Gladness* (Colorado Springs: NavPress, 1997) 165.

2. Lionel Casson, *The Horizon Book of Daily Life in Ancient Rome* (New York: American Heritage, 1975) 73.

3. Richard France, *The Gospel According to Matthew* (Grand Rapids: Eerdmans, 2002) 127.

4. Barclay, *Matthew* 166.

5. Barclay, *Matthew* 167.
6. D. Guthrie, and J. A. Motyer, eds., *The New Bible Commentary Revised* (Grand Rapids: Eerdmans, 1970) 824.
7. Bruce 1126.
8. Lewis 96.
9. France 128.
10. Lewis 96.
11. Barclay, *Matthew* 173.
12. Barclay, *Matthew* 173-175.
13. Keener 440.
14. Barker and Kohlenberger, *New Testament* 587.
15. William Barclay, *The Letter to the Romans* (Philadelphia: Westminster Press, 1975) 170.
16. Ann Japenga, "Forgiveness," *Health* May/June 1998: 114-116, 118, 120, 124.
17. Japenga 124.
18. Weaver 97.
19. Barker and Kohlenberger, *New Testament* 369-370.
20. Barker and Kohlenberger, *New Testament* 370.
21. Frank Pack, *The Gospel According to John, Part 2 (11:1-21:25)* (Abilene: ACU Press, 1984) 156-157.

Chapter 6 – You Can't Get There from Here

1. "Public Life Quotes," 6 Oct 2005 <http://www.hillwatch.com/PPRC/Quotes/Public_Life.aspx>.
2. Charles W. Keysor, *Forgiveness is a Two-Way Street* (Wheaton, IL: Victor Books, 1982) 69.
3. Smedes 148.
4. Weaver and Furlong 111
5. Weaver and Furlong 144.
6. Enright 153.
7. Enright 140.
8. Enright 158.
9. McCullough, Sandage and Worthington 223.
10. McCullough, Sandage and Worthington 222-223.
11. Worthington 77.
12. Worthington 77.
13. Paul Meier, Stephen Arterburn, and Frank Minirth, *Mastering Your Moods: Understanding Your Emotional Highs and Lows* (Nashville: Thomas Nelson, 1999) 206-207.
14. Ensor 82-84.

Chapter 7 – Shedding Your Baggage

1. "Sentence Sermons," Green's Lake Road Church of Christ Bulletin 8 Aug. 2004: 2.

2. Ruth N. Koch and Kenneth C. Haugk, *Speaking the Truth in Love: How to Be An Assertive Christian* (St. Louis: Stephen Ministries, 1992) 133.

3. Edna Pendergrass, *Help Yourself to Happiness* (Nashville: Christian Communications, 1988) 64.

4. Enright 162.

5. Eamon Tobin, *How to Forgive Yourself and Others: Steps to Reconciliation* (Liguori, MO: Liguori Publications, 1993) 21.

6. Enright 165.

7. Kay Arthur, Jill Briscoe, and Carole Mayhall, *Can a Busy Christian Develop Her Spiritual Life? Answers to Questions Women Ask About Spirituality* (Minneapolis: Bethany House, 1994) 162-163.

8. Arthur, Briscoe and Mayhall 163.

9. Pendergrass 65.

10. Colbert 134.

11. Colbert 134-135.

12. Enright 166-169.

13. Wendell Winkler, *Heart Diseases and Their Cure* (Tuscaloosa, Ala.: Winkler Publications, 1972) 6.

14. Worthington 108-109.

15. Jeffress 137.

16. Ron Lee Davis and James D. Denney, *A Forgiving God in an Unforgiving World* (Eugene: Harvest House Publishers, 1984) 159-160.

17. Jane McWhorter, *Friendship: Handle with Care* (Nashville: Gospel Advocate Co., 1999) 183.

Chapter 8 – Maneuvering Around the Potholes

1. Helen W. Kooiman, *Forgiveness in Action* (New York: Hawthorn Books, 1974) 71.

2. Roy Merritt, *Potholes: Ups and Downs on Zambia's Mission Road* (Beamsville, Ontario, Canada: Gospel Herald Foundation, 2001) 102-103.

3. Ensor 40.

4. Jeffress 144.

5. Enright 112.

6. Enright 111.

7. Ensor 131-132.

8. Comay and Brownrigg 240.

9. Keener 298.

10. Jeffress 145.

11. Davis and Denney 34-35.

12. Robert W. Harvey and David G. Benner. *Choosing the Gift of Forgiveness: How to Overcome Hurts and Brokenness* (Grand Rapids: Baker, 1996) 84-85, 88.

13. Davis and Denney 35.

14. Jeffress 132.

15. Chuck Lynch, *I Should Forgive, But ...* (Nashville: Word, 1998) 27.

16. Jeffress 133-135.

Chapter 9 – Lost and Going in Circles

1. Barclay, *Matthew* 192-193.

2. Keener 95.

3. Barker and Kohlenberger, *New Testament* 86.

4. Lawrence O. Richards, *The Teacher's Commentary* (Wheaton, IL: Victor Books, 1987) 451-453.

5. Kenneth L. Barker and John R. Kohlenberger III, eds., *Zondervan NIV Bible Commentary Vol. 1: Old Testament* (Grand Rapids: Zondervan, 1994) 1407-8.

6. Homer Hailey, *A Commentary on the Minor Prophets* (Religious Supply Inc., 1993) 137.

7. Barker and Kohlenberger, *Old Testament* 1408.

8. Barker and Kohlenberger, *Old Testament* 1408.

9. John H. Walton, Victor H. Matthews, and Mark W. Chavalas, *The IVP Bible Background Commentary: Old Testament* (Downers Grove, Ill.: InterVarsity, 2000) 753.

10. Richards 451-452.

11. Worthington 112.

12. Worthington 112-113.

13. Harvey and Benner 79-80.

14. Keener 417.

15. Barker and Kohlenberger, *New Testament* 528.

16. Spiros Zodhiates, *The Complete Word Study Dictionary: New Testament* (Chattanooga, Tenn.: AMG Publishers, 1992) 1103:3860.II.

Part Three – On the Road Again

1. "About the Film: America's First Road Trip," 6 Oct 2005 <http://www.pbs.org/horatio/about/>.

Chapter 10 – The U-Turn

1. Haney 125.

2. B. H. Dement, "Repent," *International Standard Bible Encyclopedia vol. 4* (Grand Rapids: Eerdmans, 1988) 135-136.

3. Craig Spychalla, "Encounter with Dahmer Changed Minister's Life," *Christian Chronicle* Jan. 2005: 27.

4. Roy Ratcliff, "The Gospel is for All: The Baptism of Jeffrey Dahmer," *Christian Woman* Mar/Apr 1995: 16.

5. Ratcliff 16.

6. Vern McLellan, *Shredded Wit* (Eugene, Oregon: Harvest House, 1988) 57.

7. Keener 58.

8. Jeffress 79-80.

9. Lewis 57-59.

Chapter 11 – Patching Things Up

1. "Henry Boye Quotes," Brainyquote.com 6 Oct 2005 <http://www.brainyquote.com/quotes/quotes/h/henryboye173044.html >.

2. "Model T: In Cooleemee the Model T was the King of the Road," 6 Oct 2005 <http://members.tripod.com/~cooleemee/modelt.html>.

3. "Model T."

4. "McLean County History & Genealogy News," 9 Oct 2003 Euleen Rickard, 6 Oct 2005 <http://www.geocities.com/mcleancountymuseum/100903.html>.

5. "McLean County."

6. Colbert 167.

7. Keener 232-233.

8. William Barclay, *The Gospel of Luke* (Philadelphia: Westminster Press, 1975) 205.

9. Keener 233.

10. Keener 233.

11. Barker and Kohlenberger, *New Testament* 264.

12. Barker and Kohlenberger, *New Testament* 264.

13. Keener 233.

14. Keener 233.

15. Barker and Kohlenberger, *New Testament* 264.

16. Morris 244.

17. Dale and Juanita Ryan, *Receiving Forgiveness from God* (Downers Grove, Ill.: InterVarsity Press, 2001) 47.

18. Una Kroll, *Forgive and Live* (London: Mowbray, 2000) 93-94.

19. Jeffress 127-130.

Chapter 12 – Restoring Something Worth Saving

1. Warren Wiersbe, *God Isn't In a Hurry: Learning to Slow Down and Live* (Grand Rapids: Baker, 1994) 102.

2. John T. Willis, *First and Second Samuel* (Abilene, Texas: ACU Press, 1984) 346.

3. Bruce 591.

4. Guthrie and Motyer 483.

5. H. C. Leupold, *Exposition of the Psalms* (Grand Rapids: Baker, 1975) 404.

6. Guthrie and Motyer 483.

7. Leupold 404.

8. Barker and Kohlenberger, *Old Testament* 854.

9. Bruce 592.

10. Morris 146.

11. Anthony Lee Ash, *The Gospel According to Luke: Part 1, 1:1-9:50* (Austin, Texas: Sweet, 1972) 135.

12. Ash 135

13. Ash 136.

14. Morris 148.

15. Morris 148-149.

16. William Barclay, *The Letter to the Hebrews* (Philadelphia: Westminster Press, 1977) 116-117.

17. Barker and Kohlenberger, *New Testament* 986.

Chapter 13 – The Last Few Miles

1. Clarissa Pinkola Estes, *Women Who Run With the Wolves* (London: Rider, 1992) 369.

2. Enright 224-225, 236.

3. Enright 225-232.

4. Weaver and Furlong 105.

5. Worthington 208.

6. Smedes 134-135.

7. Smedes 137.

8. Smedes 137.

9. Enright 200.

10. Enright 200.

11. Estes 372-373.

Make Your Bible Study Time Count.
Try one of these popular favorites from Nancy Eichman.

Seasoning Your Words

If you ever have trouble controlling your tongue, saying something you shouldn't or failing to say something you should, then this practical and easy-to-understand study is for you. This popular book has sold more than 35,000 copies, making it a perennial favorite.
0-89225-463-7

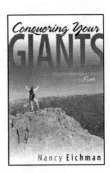

Conquering Your Giants

Are your everyday fears preventing you from living life to its fullest? Learn how to face your giants and be victorious with God's help in Nancy Eichman's 13-week ladies Bible class book, *Conquering Your Giants*.
0-89225-532-3

Keeping Your Balance

It has been said that one out of four Americans is imbalanced. Eichman tells us to look to Jesus to find out how to have a balanced life — mentally, emotionally and spiritually.
0-89225-472-6

God's Makeover Plan

In this book, Eichman searches the Scriptures to see how a makeover in our attitudes can produce changes in our inner and outer selves.
0-89225-380-0

Printed in the United States
94018LV00005B/229-285/A